CHALLENGE YOURSELF AND WIN YOUR BEST FUTURE

SMART START CHALLENGE Handbook

First Edition

"When you know what the rules are and what you need to do to win, then it just takes practice to make it a reality." Kirsten Peck

As a teacher, I have studied the best strategies or practices to follow if you want to be successful in life. Anybody can learn the skills necessary for better jobs and more money, but everybody has to practice those skills to improve. Intelligence is something that is developed in your brain and once you tap into that power, nothing can stop you!

This Smart Start Challenge was created for students who may be struggling or are not sure how to make their dreams come true. I want to be the teacher that helps you unlock your hidden potential. Join with me in our virtual classroom and push yourself to greatness!

Can You Spend A Month To Create Your Dream Life?

The Early Reviews Are Coming In...

"Ms. Peck has such a good vibe, she makes me smile and feel confident. I loved the twist of the book and the Catalyst For Change project. Every day was something different but it all added up to a new outlook on life". Georgia Dupree, 15 years old

"Ms. Peck shares the info that a lot of people need to hear. She's real and tells you things you need to use in life every day. It's the stuff that got missed in school or my parents never told me. My view of my future has changed after these 31 days". Nathan Walton, 17 years old

"Within the Challenge, the Catalyst For Change project is exactly what is needed for struggling students. It gives teens information, allows them to see beyond their own world, and empowers them to use their voice. The project weaves in perfectly with the other lessons and "coaching" they're getting. The entire process breeds confidence and engages students with their educational goals and ultimately, a better future". Dr. Diane Goldstein, Retired Superintendent, Kalamazoo County Schools, Michigan

"This challenge is timely and absolutely necessary for today's teens struggling with achieving their academic goals, or who have lack of confidence in themselves. I truly think Ms. Peck has tapped into something that will be transformational for teens, and their parents, because it allows them to have ownership of their goals and ultimately their future". Lee Mariano, Founder & CEO, Alexidom Coaching, Virginia

"Ms. Peck's Smart Start Challenge is an engaging, yet virtual event of personal growth activities developed for struggling high school students. The daily 15 minute lessons with a favorite teacher puts the student in the driver seat with individualized exercises. The point system keeps students accountable for/to themselves which builds self-confidence and motivates them to continue making positive choices for all the aspects of their daily life". Nancy Miritello, 30+ year Veteran Teacher and Behavior Specialist, Pinellas County Schools, Florida

The Smart Start Challenge Handbook

WIN MS. PECK'S VIDEO AWARD WITH PRIDE

This month will challenge your beliefs and test your ability to make a difference in our world. You get to pick the social issue that you feel is most urgent to change. There are so many, whichever you are most passionate about is the best choice. We are going to use the power of social media for good with this project. Thank you in advance from the people we can help with a little brain power and a lot of heart. Let's do this!! Ms. Peck

TABLE OF CONTENTS

TABLE OF CONTENTS

Make The Commitment

Ms. Peck's SMART START CHALLENGE will be the most amazing month of your life!

Congratulations to you for deciding to get all the insider info and major details you need to be successful today, and every day of your life. This challenge will help you discover things about yourself and help you start every day smarter.

15 Minutes a Day, Every Day = A Smart Start to Your Future

When you accept this CHALLENGE, you are going to practice thinking skills and build mental strength to get a smarter start in your life. It is critical that you build a strong foundation today because it will help you build the future of your dreams. The earlier you begin dreaming and setting plans into action, the earlier you will be successful.

Every day you will simply spend 15 minutes reading and thinking about what you want out of life then, plan and work to achieve it. Having a great life sounds difficult, but it can be done easily; 15 minutes a day, every day.

When you put your mind to something, you can make it happen. This simple habit is one that will bring you great wealth and happiness in the future. It is a concept that has proven true throughout the years. Critical thinking is a skill that always leads to rewards.

It is so important to adopt a growth mindset and enjoy learning. If you have experienced a bad situation at school, I want to say I'm sorry to you. I also want you to let that go and focus on today and moving forward. You can have some incredible brain training with Ms. Peck and get a whole new attitude.

31 Days Will Transform Your World

If you know how to think your way out of difficult situations, you will be better off for it. Yes, I am talking about money and being richer, but also in your relationships with people.

Being able to stop and think about a solution is a life skill everyone needs. Having smarts is important and you get them by working your brain, thinking.

Yes, that's right. Developing your intelligence is just like building up arm muscles. The brain is a muscle and the more you use it, the stronger and faster it can work. These middle and high school years are important because you can get a solid foundation now and build upon it for a lifetime. Learning new skills that open doors to your future is available to you right now.

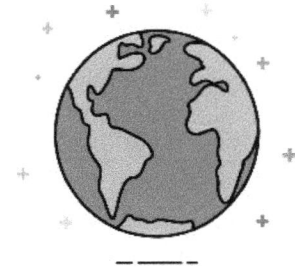

I challenge you to get your smartest life started NOW!

Do not wait another day to begin your best life. The younger a person is, the greater their potential for greatness, at least that's what this SMART START CHALLENGE is about.

Let's Get Started - Make a List of Champions You Admire Here

What Is YOUR Challenge?

Listen up! The clock is ticking, and your life is ahead of you.

I've seen it all and heard lots of unreal, but totally true stories from students over the years. As a teacher, I have found a way to help students get a grip on their situation (whatever it is) and realize that they control their future. I teach students that their life is under their control. It seems so easy and obvious but trust me, every struggling, unhappy teenager I meet says it is impossible, but when they try it... it works! Every time.

For those of you who are happy and feeling confident about school, I want to congratulate you for reaching this point in your education. For you, this SMART START CHALLENGE will be about your decision to take life to the next level. How far can you go with your dreams? What type of future are you going to have? The challenge is within each of us to be our best.

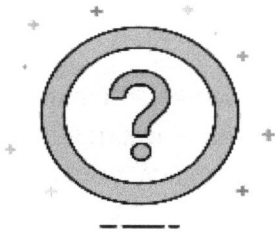

Whether up or down, everyone knows "Teenagerhood" can be brutal. You are at a stage in life where you're changing into a young adult. Your hormones are doing crazy things. For many, school could be the worst part because most of the time, it's difficult to concentrate, thanks to the hormones. Maybe the Math teacher talks too quickly, seems to skip some steps and then magically comes up with an answer while you are wondering ... "what did they say?"

Perhaps, it's not the subjects that you are worried about at school. You are worried about being popular and people joking about your weight. You have tried everything, but you just can't get in shape. Maybe you are battling acne. You've tried the creams and every DIY you see on YouTube, but it won't go away.

The truth is, you are beautiful on the inside and that is what is important.

Or maybe there's this boy or girl you've got a massive crush on, but they are super popular in school and you're not. So, it makes sense that you are sad all the time. School can seem like the worst kind of punishment ever. You wish you didn't have to go. And now, this digital learning is a whole new, unknown mystery at school.

Maybe you know so much about a lot of things that others just make fun of it. They push you down in the hallways and no one will sit with you at lunchtime. You wish you knew how to make school work right. Well, finally you have asked Ms. Peck to help and this SMART START CHALLENGE is going to change your world.

You are faced with difficult situations daily, where you must make tough choices. A few times, you make good choices while other times, you don't. You may struggle with being online or gaming and those habits prevent you from being as productive as you need to be.

Now that Covid-19 has taken over the world, it probably feels even more out of control. You are not alone; many people are feeling "out of sorts". Yes, the world is shaken up with a virus, but it does not have to feel that way all the time.

Maybe you feel like you want to talk about it, but you're not sure who will listen. You don't want to be judged. You just want someone to understand, and maybe help you. You want someone to hold your hand and tell you it's going to be okay – even though you don't think it will. You must end that stinking thinking and Ms. Peck knows exactly what to do.

I know it can feel like you are living a nightmare right now, but I also know that it can be fixed. You don't have to keep feeling like this. You don't have to keep struggling with schoolwork like you are now. You also don't have to keep hiding in the shadows. I know there is an amazing kid inside you, and it is time to let them out!

THIS CHALLENGE WAS MADE JUST FOR YOU

With a little help from me, you will be able to reach in deep, discover and show the rest of the world who you really are. Every teenager goes through these growing pains. It does not have to be so difficult. Together, we will sort out whatever your challenge may be and tell your story in the most awesome way possible!

With 31 days of a little motivation and lots of interesting activities, you are going to be forming better success-oriented habits. With these smart habits, you are going to tackle a big problem that concerns you and you will be proud of the work you can accomplish.

Because of the Catalyst for Change project, you will feel stronger in every area of your life. With a little practice and coaching, you will be able to get your grades on track and start enjoying school. Ms. Peck can even help you adjust to going to school online.

I know you can accomplish great things and it starts right here. I challenge you to find your superpowers and direction toward your best future. I am going to cheer you on to victory this month and into the rest of your amazing life. I am coaching you with the little steps to make great progress and looking forward to working together!

Ms. Peck

Now It's Your Turn - Write a note to yourself about what you want to change and make better in your life and world. What do you think needs to improve? What does your "Dream Life" look like?

Rules Of Life According To Ms. Peck

"When you know what the rules are and what you need to do to win, then it just takes practice to make it a reality". Ms. Peck

As a teacher, I have studied the best strategies or practices to follow if you want to be successful in life. Anybody can learn the skills necessary for better jobs and more money, but everybody must practice those skills to improve. Intelligence is something that is developed in your brain and once you tap into that power, nothing can stop you!

The SMART START CHALLENGE begins with these best practices for you to use every day as your new ground rules to life. Read this out loud and start getting these ideas into your memory. You agreed to the idea of training your brain and making it smarter. Here are the ground rules to getting through this marathon month and kick-start your future.

If you get distracted, this list will help refocus you on what you want to achieve. It takes time to develop your genius. I know practice makes perfect, and I know when you find the special magic, anything is possible. Studies have shown it takes 10,000 hours of practice to reach true mastery of a skill like basketball or piano. Anyone can do it, beginning with just 15 minutes a day.

Rule #1 - Use Every Day to Improve Yourself

Every day, you get new information and you think about it in new ways. Your brain needs time to think about the info and daily repeated actions develop mental strength. Brain training works. When you spend 15 minutes working on creative ideas or critical thinking, things can only get better in your life. Only you can take those steps toward your new attitude and life, every day, no excuses.

Rule #2 Practice Writing Daily to Communicate Your Ideas

Consider this SMART START CHALLENGE as your virtual connection to your favorite teacher and you are learning the insider info. Even without "live" feedback, these daily activities will guide you toward success. You need practice writing and there's no way to improve without doing it, so get your pen and paper, or laptop, ready for action.

The daily workouts include reading and practicing critical thinking skills which needs to be written down. The space in the handbook is the guide for you to fill in or write in the margins and space in the back. Feel free to expand onto paper or digital however you wish. The expectation is that you will write sentences or paragraphs as prompted in the activities in a readable quality.

Rule #3 The Scorecard and Points Always Matter

What kind of challenge would this be without points and a scorecard?? Just like in real life, you must know what you have to do to earn those points. Whatever the prize is, be it trophies, cash bonuses or large salaries, in order to win, you must score the points.

- Every day you will earn points for working out and meeting deadlines.
- Every day, while practicing good communication skills, you get the opportunity to make bank toward your future.
- Every response is worth points on the scorecard, so putting in your best effort will always lead to improvement and growth.

There is a checklist at the end of every day's work out. Building integrity means you must be honest with yourself and score the skills you practice each day. You will earn points by doing these things:

- Personal care practices
- Daily questions and exercises
- Meeting weekly target goals
- Catalyst For Change project milestones.

Rule #4 - Give It Your Best and Make the Commitment

Sure, you can cheat and add points without putting in effort, but you know that's not really going to work in the long run. It seems so obvious, but if you have the bad habit of doing just enough to get by, that bad habit must end. Think about it, would you put cheap gasoline into a racecar?? NO!

When you make the commitment to work daily at your best effort, every action you take pays off in your future. Look at your schedule and decide a time of day when you will work on the CHALLENGE. Write it down, tell your friends you are busy and set your alarm daily to make it easy to remember. When you finish the SMART START CHALLENGE, you will be rewarded greatly for every effort you've made.

Challenge Overview

Every day we work on a different area and focus on improving specific skills.

It is called a distributed practice when you separate activities out and repeat them to improve them. You know, just like if you have batting practice every day and weight training only three times a week. Over time, your skills and muscles get stronger and it seems much easier to accomplish. Here is the guide to the icons and each daily topic. Check them off and add them up as you practice.

Daily Practice

Weekly Coaching Rounds

Mindfulness

Problem Solving

My Self

Academics

Communications

Catalyst For Change

Self-care Is Critical To Getting a Smart Start

Taking good care of yourself seems obvious but we don't always do it. This is your gentle reminder that a balanced diet of nutritional foods is the fuel your body burns. Also, do not forget about exercise and how much your body has to move around.

Drinking water is also on the list of things to do every day. Also, pay a little more attention to how much sleep you are getting. Experts recommend 8-9 hours. When you keep score at the end of each day, no points if you get less than 7 hours of sleep at night.

Self-care also includes how you treat your heart or spirit. It is about being nice to yourself, having a positive attitude and doing your best to learn the most you can. Showing appreciation or faith in a higher power are also included on the daily to-do list.

I also want to include the need to give up all addictions you may be experiencing. Many teens are engaging in repeated behaviors that may seem innocent to begin with, but are dangerous in the long-run. It is important to get a grip on compulsive behavior now, before it escalates. This includes things like self-harm, alcohol or drug use, but also body/food issues and gaming/social media addiction.

This CHALLENGE will give you confidence within yourself to power past any of these bad habits.

How do you rest or take care of yourself? List 3 ways you treat yourself like Royalty – the King or Queen you are!

Daily Scorecard

Just like in a ball game, you have to keep track of the ups and downs to know when you win the game.

Being in this CHALLENGE is going to make you feel incredible and smarter because you can accomplish these exercises every day. You will see improvements in your body and in your future. This will help you push yourself past any limits starting right now.

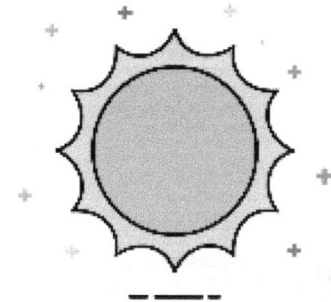

Here is the tool that will help you focus on reaching your best future. This is the scoring breakdown for all the activities that are part of the SMART START CHALLENGE. Every day you will rate your participation using this scoring system.

You get points for taking care of yourself with healthy daily practices. The clock starts on Day #1 with physical and mental activities related to these points. Good nutrition, some exercise and plenty of water are obvious. After your workout, rate yourself with this scorecard. Yes, training your brain means you have to do the math!

The practice is easy to follow. If you are doing schoolwork on the weekend, then give yourself the 2 points (+1 for attendance). To recognize the things you are thankful for, write down 2-3 words in the space after "Gratitude" and if your "Attitude" is looking forward and upward, then you score those points. Be honest with yourself, it takes practice and time for your new "Growth Mindset" to kick-in!

1 Point for Each	Diet - Fitness - Water - Sleep - Attendance - Gratitude	
2 Points for Each	Attitude - Schoolwork - Warm-up Questions	Add It Up!
5 Points for Each	Daily Exercises	
10 Points	SMART Wakeup	DEPOSIT TOTAL FOR TODAY
BONUS Points	SMART Tasks	MY POINTS =

**Don't worry - I have given you samples below the activity to target and score your work.

Expectations for Daily Warm-up Questions

To earn the most points, you need to answer all 5 questions at 2 points each. The responses need to restate the question in the answer. It needs to include an example or details to demonstrate thinking and expression of your ideas. Yes, these are like the requirements for academic writing. Imagine sending your work to your favorite teacher. I know you will do your best.

STUDENT SAMPLE TARGET: Taken From Day #5, Warmup Question #1 - What is your toughest challenge at school?

"My biggest challenge at school is how boring it is every day. The teachers stink and waste time with busy work about nothing important. I hate going there every day."

Why Does This Score The Full 2 Points?

- It restates the question by using the same words, "my challenge at school is…"
- It gives an example and details, "bad teachers" and "nothing important"
- It makes a statement from their point of view – they are not happy.
- 3 sentences is acceptable length. Full paragraphs in SMART Tasks need more details making them 5+ sentences long.

Expectations for BONUS or SMART Tasks

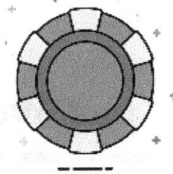

The second way to score points is to complete the SMART Tasks and BONUS token opportunities. Pay attention to the instructions for each day and be ready to show off your skills. SMART Tasks will include a sample for you to use as a guide when you score your points at the end of your workout.

During this month, you will see how this daily practice gets easier and your communication will improve. Believe me, this writing practice is critical to your success in the CHALLENGE. There is space here to write but I encourage you to expand onto paper/laptop to get the most benefit from working every day. I also suggest you get a nice smooth writing pen or package of markers to boost your energy, writing in bright colors is fun!

Be sure that you bring your best level of competition to your SMART START CHALLENGE. The more you put into things, the greater their payoff. I know you can create an amazing Catalyst for Change project where all your work will be rewarded!

Track The Stats

Challenge yourself to do better every day and watch your rewards add up.

Report Your Daily Scores Here

Day 1	Day 2	Day 3	Day 4	Day 5	Day 6	Day 7
Day 8	Day 9	Day 10	Day 11	Day 12	Day 13	Day 14
Day 15	Day 16	Day 17	Day 18	Day 19	Day 20	Day 21
Day 22	Day 23	Day 24	Day 25	Day 26	Day 27	Day 28
Day 29	Day 30	Day 31				

You have 10 SMART Tasks To Complete

Check Off Each Weekly Round

It is important to keep score daily, and these stats charts will keep you focused on the end game and how well you are doing. Start adding it up weekly as you work through each round of virtual coaching. Round after round, just like a championship tournament. You will have the most rewarding feeling, in 31 quick days from now, when you recount for your final score.

☑	ADD UP WEEKLY SCORE HERE	SMART BONUS DONE	ADD WEEKLY BONUS EARNED	WEEKLY SUBTOTALS
ROUND #1		4 Tasks	Finish Days 1-7 = 25+ points	
ROUND #2		1 Task	Finish Days 1-15 = 50+ points	
ROUND #3		1 Task	Finish Days 1-21 = 75+ points	
ROUND #4		3 Tasks	Finish Days 1-28 = 100+ points	
KNOCKOUT ROUND #5		1 Task		**FINAL TOTAL HERE**

ON YOUR MARK, GET READY...

YOU NEED TO KNOW THE TOTAL NUMBER OF

POINTS AVAILABLE IS 1,895

WHAT IS YOUR TARGET POINT GOAL? _____

YES, YOU CAN MAKE THOSE TARGETS!

Lists are a great tool to use -
Make a list of things you want
to accomplish this next year.

Here's the Opening Bell - OK GO!

I am excited to hear about your progress and invite you to join me on the website -
SmartStartChallenge.com

I also want to encourage you to promote your ideas for improving our world in the Catalyst for Change project.
You can find me on various social media platforms and share your ideas with me and the world! This is going to
be so much fun!! Ms. Peck

Day 1 - Finding Direction

Warm-up Questions:

1. What do you like doing? Make a list.
2. What are you good at? Why are you good at doing it? Explain.
3. What do you want to learn more about? Make a list.
4. What kind of person do you want to be by next year? Describe.
5. Have you thought about what you want to do after high school? Explain.

Power Vocab: Direction, Dreams

Direction: The course or path on which something is moving or pointing towards.

Dreams: Imagination of the future, or things you really want to have or achieve.

Lesson:

What you do every day depends heavily on where you're going in the long run. If you have a flight to catch at 11:30am, you would leave for the airport by 9:00am because you'd need to check in and go through security before you board the plane. It's not the same if you're taking a bus to school. For the bus, you could leave your house and walk casually to the bus stop at 11:15am and you'd still be early.

Our direction in life is the same thing!

If you don't figure out where you want to go, you will make a lot of wrong choices or turns along the way. Many times, you could easily end up in the wrong place or time. Imagine missing the start of a movie or going to a party that is not happening at the friend's house you went to. Frustrating right?

This is why you should start thinking early about what you want to do or what you want to become. Your "vision of your future" is something that is going to grow and change over the years, don't panic or think that it is forever established. Some people seem to fall into their natural calling, some people take more time.

To me, your future is something you urgently need to focus on finding because if you do not have one, you will get further down the road of life without even knowing which road you are on. If you begin to explore different careers or work opportunities now, you will know what interests you or which directions you want to go in.

Right now, you probably are not sure what you want. Or do you? Maybe you want to get better grades, or you want to try out for the soccer team. I'm guessing you also want to get better in other areas of your life. Maybe you want to have a better relationship with your parents or discover what really captures your imagination and dreams of greatness.

When you think about it and choose the things you do, it helps you make the right decisions and be smarter. You will only do things that bring you closer to your dreams. You will also stay away from people or habits that can distract you from getting to where you want to be.

One key thing you have to know is that it is up to YOU to make your dreams come true. You, and you alone, are in charge of your life.

The sooner that sinks in, the easier a lot of things will be for you. Many people like to blame others for their failures. But they don't realize that the responsibility to do well is 100% theirs.

This is why life coaching is important. Coaching (and this type of Challenge) opens your eyes to the things you are capable of. It doesn't let you make excuses for laziness. Rather, it pushes you to keep giving your best until you see the results you desire.

You are going to begin to set your goals or dreams in motion right now. Be smart about it. By that I mean, set dreams that you can pinpoint. You can start dreaming by saying something like this: "I love dogs and want to be a veterinarian." Think about everything that interests you and consider why you would like that type of career or business.

When you start to think about why these ideas are important to you, something magical will happen. If you understand the emotions and success you desire, you can make specific long-term goals to achieve ANYTHING!!

Nothing will stop you when you have your goals set and plans made.

DAY 1 - FINDING DIRECTION

When you have a big dream, you can break that into smaller, more measurable goals and things to do. You could say: "I'm going to really study in my science classes this year and volunteer at an animal shelter."

Then, give it a timeframe and find any resources you need or get past any obstacles in your way. "So, if this is my dream, then I also need to start looking at college requirements and career paths with my guidance counselor before signing up for classes next semester."

A major part of this idea of finding your direction includes thinking about your personal values or principles or morals. They have different names but the point is, you have an underlying emotion or reason for you to want something. Values are those things that guide what you do and why you do them.

When you examine the values and take the time to feel the emotions and judge them, you will begin to understand why you dream of being a veterinarian (for example). Values are part of the mixture you need to tap into your superpowers or mojo. They give you the energy you need to get to your incredible future.

Exercise #1 - Values Clarification

Read this list, evaluate each value and the importance to you and your future. Circle the 10 most important to you.

Love	Wealth	Knowledge	Fairness	Humor	Friends
Free time	Morals	Family	Creativity	Peace	Nature
Calmness	Beauty	Adventure	Safety	Honesty	Popularity
Respect	Responsibility	Variety	Recognition	Wisdom	Achievement
Success	Independence	Spirituality	Loyalty	Stability	Fun

Of these 10 values, eliminate the 5 you consider to be less important compared to the other 5. When you make this cut in half, it means you must look deeper into your soul and feelings. What are you willing to sacrifice to make something else happen? Write the 5 most important words in the spaces below:

_____   _____   _____   _____   _____

This first step of examining what makes you unique is asking "what makes you who you are?" When you understand what's driving you toward or away from something, you become smarter about how you use your energy. Take each of these words and write a sentence that explain your thinking and reasoning about what each of the values means to you. Only you know why it matters to you. This type of critical thinking work is difficult but very meaningful to your success.

1. _____

2. _____

3. _____

4. _____

5. _____

DAY 1 - FINDING DIRECTION

Exercise #2 - Create Your Mission Statement - SMART Task

We talked earlier about having dreams and goals and how they help you make better choices every day. In this exercise, you are going to bring it all together into your personal, success-focused mission statement.

A mission statement is what you are all about. It is not only what you are setting out to achieve, but why it matters. To write a great mission statement, think about what you want to do or where you want to be, and what you will have as your reward.

Simply identify the things you are interested in and what you love doing. When you are a teenager, anything is possible, so DREAM BIG!! Next, include the values or reasoning which will energize you toward your future. What do you get out of it when you reach your dream? When you answer the question of what matters to you, you will be able to achieve it.

Here is an example of a mission statement:

"My mission is to become a veterinarian because I enjoy taking responsibility for my dog and feeling the love when my pet is healthy and happy."

For this teenager, life now seems easier and they are smarter, making better decisions to reach their vision of the future. The statement also recognizes responsibility and love that is the reward for the hard work along the way. Every time that dog gets a walk, the teen feels stronger about the future. When the teen faces a problem or difficult situation, they will be better prepared and know what to do.

Other mission statements from teenagers:

Amber - "Expressing my creativity helps me to grow new ideas."

Whitney – "Care, Love, Fight, Truth."

Tony – "I accept nothing less than my best from myself."

Joseph – "My passion for basketball teaches me focus and strengthens me on and off the court."

Hannah – "Honesty and loyalty are my greatest strengths and demands I put on myself, for myself."

Let's get your thinking going now, finish these sentence starters, or brainstorm a list:

- **My greatest abilities are...**

- **My interests are...**

- **I feel inspired by...**

- **If I could do anything I would....**

- **The people I admire are (List their names and why you admire them)**

Now, close your eyes and breathe. This is for you, so don't worry about a teacher grading it, or anyone reading it. Scribble your ideas all over in the margins. Take a chance on yourself and dig deep to think about the future you want to have.

Your mission statement will change over time, but it will guide your choices and the habits you form. When you have your mission statement, you have a map to your future. It helps you think clearly and make decisions that create your vision of the future, in real life.

DAY 1 - FINDING DIRECTION

Ok, write it all out in a sentence or two. Try to merge your passion or inspiration with why it matters to you. What do you want your life to be like? Maybe you should look at those 5 values you selected and select the two that are most important. Start thinking and writing out your ideas.

Write yours below: - My mission is to _____

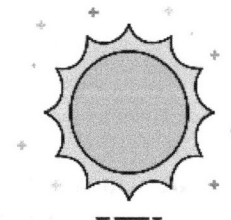

You have done an awesome job working today on a difficult subject. Doing critical thinking about yourself takes a lot of energy and personal accountability. Be honest with your self-evaluation, your future depends upon it. The challenge is on!

Here Is Your First Scorecard

1 Point for Each	Diet - Fitness - Water - Sleep - Attendance - Gratitude	
2 Points for Each	Attitude - Schoolwork - Warm-up Questions	**Add It Up!**
5 Points for Each	Daily Exercises	
10 Points	SMART Wakeup	
BONUS Points	SMART Tasks	

DEPOSIT TOTAL FOR TODAY

MY POINTS =

SMART Tasks +25 points = Mission Statement Completed

First, fill in something you are thankful for in the space next to GRATITUDE. You will begin the SMART Wakeup tomorrow, so those 10 points are not available today. But, you do have the SMART Task points to include in the scoring. Check or circle each point you earned. Once you have everything added up, go back to Track the Stats on page 20 and report your score.

Be sure to check off the first SMART Task in Round #1 as being done also.

Coaching Tip From Ms. Peck —

Today's SMART Task needs to come from your heart. It should be a statement that reflects your spirit and dreams. A mission statement will change, but with a good one you can touch your inner being and know what to do in almost any situation. It might take some time to really develop yours but writing one today earns you those SMART Task bonus points!

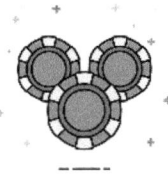

I want you to know that part of my "Mission" is to shake up your thinking about school and how things are going. A disruption is something that causes a shift or break from the normal. I designed this handbook to be read sideways because I wanted to get you to open it and read it. It looks different, it will help you think differently. I also made big fonts to be easy to read and added funny icons as symbolism. I know every one of them will click in your head and add extra meaning.

They say you should never judge a book by the cover and that is very true. Always look inside and investigate before you make a decision. I hope this CHALLENGE handbook and our "virtual classroom" will help you see things differently. You will have a smarter outlook on life and what you want out of it. That's my mission.

Day 2 - Get A Growth Mindset

Warm-up Questions:

1. What challenges do you face at school?
2. How do you react to difficult situations?
3. What kind of attitude do you have most days?
4. What makes your attitude happen the way it does?
5. What things are you doing to become the kind of person you want to become?

Power Words: Growth, Habit

Growth: The process of growing or progressive development.

Habit: Something that a person does often in a regular and repeated way. It could also mean a type of behavior that is learned and practiced till it becomes involuntary.

Lesson:

As we grow older, our bodies get bigger and stronger and our minds change as well. The things we enjoyed when we were younger like playing with dolls or building blocks no longer interest us. As we age, we want to try new things, or things that are a lot more difficult or grown-up. Growing in your bodies is obvious but understanding how your mind grows is harder to see. Meta-cognition, or being mindful, means we are thinking about how we think so we can learn and grow from it.

Today, we need to understand and grow in our attitude towards tackling problems and handling situations. Think about a 3-year-old whose shoelaces are untied. She may feel overwhelmed and cry, but you wouldn't. You would reach down and tie those laces because you know how to get it done.

When faced with a daunting task, do you always ask yourself: "how do I make this work out"? Rather than saying "I can't do this", do you ask, "how do I learn this"? When you ask questions that focus on the solution, you are teaching your mind to become smarter and to think better.

Achieving results by tackling problems can be difficult but often is quite rewarding. Think about when you finally crossed that difficult level in your favorite game. Or when you fit the pieces together for that giant jigsaw puzzle. You felt really great – like you had accomplished something remarkable. You know you can do it again and you will.

What if you saw your math problem as a challenge you have met before and will meet again? Rather than just panic and blank out, think of it as a difficult game or level you can meet because you did it before. It doesn't matter if the numbers have changed, use your skills to make the calculations to reach the solution, just like last time.

Anything is learnable if you put your mind to it. That's what a growth mindset does for you. When you have a growth mindset, you are never focused on how tough problems are. Instead, you choose to look at what you could learn and get smarter from those problems.

Having a growth mindset also makes you view your mistakes differently. Instead of saying terrible things to yourself if you blow it, you see every screw up as a teachable moment. It may sound funny, but how will you know if you are successful if you don't fail first?

What if you considered failure as the best way to learn from your mistakes? Imagine never really failing as long as you learn something from it. Doesn't that make failure a good thing? It is all in how you look at it, isn't it?

The Not-Even-Thinking Habits

Habits are things we do over and over, often without even thinking about it. Habits can be good or bad, depending on what they are and how they affect us. Good habits bring you closer to your dreams. They encourage you to be productive and make you a better person. It is a good habit to drink plenty of water and brush your teeth. Obvious, right?

Bad habits are negative and often make you lazy. They make you waste time and they pull you away from your dreams. They are often destructive and have horrible consequences. Believe it or not, small things like always being late, or hiding the truth can really hurt you.

DAY 2 - GET A GROWTH MINDSET

Being mindful and choosing your habits is a great way to create your future. That's because we eventually become a reflection of our habits. To make your dreams come true, you must choose to adopt and cultivate good habits. This just means that you will focus on picking and keeping habits that take you closer to your dreams. As you pick up good habits, you drop the negative habits. You are choosing, by your habits, who you want to become.

Having a growth mindset also means you choose the right habits to put yourself in your best situations. Creating a solid foundation with good habits starts first thing in the morning. Today's SMART Task is to identify the good and the bad habits that you have and use. Then, we are going to create a morning routine to jump-start your best day, for your best life.

Exercise #1 - Recognize The Habits

Think about the things you do often and consider part of your regular, daily routine. Here's a quick chart to get you thinking, but you really have to be honest with yourself and make the list that reflects the things you do without even thinking.

Good or Bad Habits -   **Use this space to make your list - Good and Bad**

Sleeping 8 hours every night   **Halo and Minecraft until 3am**

Sister is my best friend   **Fighting with my brother**

Talking out problems to fix them   **Ignoring problems, hiding the truth**

Eating healthy food and exercise   **Junk food and candy, couch potato**

What do you do every day to help yourself and make you stronger and smarter? Which habits are taking you away from your goal? Which new habits do you need to adopt? We are going to work on this throughout this month, so for right now, be honest and write them all down, good or bad.

Exercise #2 - Create A Smart Start Wakeup Routine - SMART Task

It is a proven fact that establishing a positive Growth Mindset, first thing in the morning, energizes and focuses you on success. A morning routine is like putting the best gasoline in a racecar to make sure you will zoom across the finish line.

Some people use prayers to set their minds towards happiness or peace, which is a great place for you to begin on this SMART Task. This is different from your beliefs in God or religion. This is something that includes your dreams, short term goals and values to motivate you in difficult times.

I want you to create your own personal, inspirational message for your future. Sometimes called your mantra, it is a message that will energize you and guide you toward success.

Start with your mission statement and add more to it, making it more powerful for you. It can be written as a prayer, or a poem if that matches your personality. You could also make up a rhyme or song if you want to give it a rhythm. When you repeat it daily, it will help you focus and achieve your mission statement. It does not have to be long, but it absolutely has to be personal and motivational for YOU.

The SMART Task today is to put together a specific morning wakeup routine and write it down. The experts say your routine should be written out like a script or an agenda. It includes not only your inspirational message (or mantra), but the specific self-care you do to keep your body in top condition. Because you have identified the values you feel are important, your morning routine also recognizes them as part of spirit or gratitude blessing.

A morning wakeup routine brings all three parts of a person together ---
Mind, Body and Spirit, and starts the day with unbelievable energy and focus.

Jot down a few quick ideas for your personal message:

DAY 2 - GET A GROWTH MINDSET

To help you understand the SMART Task, here's an example of a morning wakeup routine:

"Every morning, I wake up to my alarm at 7:00 and read my motivational message out loud. (insert my personal mantra here). I will do 10 jumping jacks and 10 windmill twists to wake up my body. After I get dressed, I will brush my teeth and make my bed to show gratitude for my room and home. Then, I will read my mantra out loud again and drink a big glass of water. Finally, I will pack my lunch and backpack and eat something before my second alarm goes off and I leave for school."

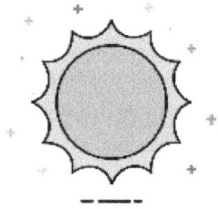

In this example, all three elements or parts come together. Do you see how the positive message is reinforced with the body and spirit of gratitude? The example works for that student, take your time to think about what little pieces of you need to be uplifted every morning. Some people use music and others like quiet peacefulness.

You will be setting the focus of your mind with this personalized mantra spoken aloud first thing in the morning. You are going to be caring for your body and recognizing your values or spirituality. Because the routine is written down, it will easily become a good habit to follow. By the end of this month, the routine will be automatic and every day will start smoothly and you will feel great.

Your morning routine may include time for working on the CHALLENGE, or you may be too rushed before going to school. It might be a good idea to use time in the afternoon or after dinner to read, think and write the daily exercises. If you make it an established appointment, you help your brain prepare for and complete the workout. Some of the power in the CHALLENGE comes from you building up endurance by working every day.

Be sure to include these items in your routine. Once you have it written down and start practicing it daily, it should take a minute or two first thing in the morning.

- Mind – Goal Setting Incantation of Focus

- Body – Energizing Wake-up of Movement

- Spirit – Positive Attitude Adjustment

Write yours now - My Smart Start Wakeup routine and daily practices for success are:

Today's Scorecard

1 Point for Each	Diet - Fitness - Water - Sleep - Attendance - Gratitude	
2 Points for Each	Attitude - Schoolwork - Warm-up Questions	**Add It Up!**
5 Points for Each	Daily Exercises	
10 Points	SMART Wakeup	
BONUS Points	SMART Tasks	

DEPOSIT TOTAL FOR TODAY
MY POINTS =

SMART Task +25 points for SMART Wakeup being created - Start earning points doing it tomorrow

Coaching Tip From Ms. Peck -

One of the goals for this month is for you to recognize your strengths and improve your focus on success. Your thoughts or your perception about the world is something you can control and use like gasoline to power your future. Burn your memory with highlights of the best days or times when you were successful.

The Wakeup routine has also been called an "In-Can-Tation "because it sets your mind on what can happen today. Focus and pay attention to the little things you do from now going forward and they will energize you to accomplish amazing things.

Reminder – Be sure to check off SMART Task #2 on your stats tracker!

Day 3 - My Internal Bank

Warm-up Questions:

1. What habits do you need to give up?
2. How do you take care of your heart?
3. What do you care most about?
4. How do you feel when you succeed at something?
5. Do you keep a daily diary to track the steps you're making towards your goals?

Power Words: Internal Bank, Scorecard

Internal Bank: A term used to describe the habits and character traits stored inside of you.

Scorecard: A report that gives information about the progress of someone or something.

Lesson:

Everyone knows banks are places where we keep money. We open accounts with them and trust them to keep our money safe. We treat our bank accounts like treasure chests filled with gold and jewels. We don't give out details about our accounts to just anyone. We only share a bit of these details with the people we trust. This is because some people are fraudulent, and we wouldn't want them to mess with our money.

People who care about us can give us money for our account. When you have a job or business, you will get paid for work you do and deposit the cash or check into your bank account. Over time, your bank account should be growing in value.

The most amazing thing is, even though we're giving our money to the bank, we still have full control and 24/7 access to it. So, whenever you want your money; you can make a withdrawal as long as you have up to that amount to take out. If you don't have the money, they give you a penalty, called an overdraft, which takes more of your money away from you.

Today's lesson is about the idea of an internal bank inside each and every one of us. Every day, we make deposits with positive things like healthy meals and plenty of sleep. We also make withdrawals with our bad habits or stress or anger.

Just like the bank, in life, you can only take out what you put in or what's in your account. If you put in junk or stuff that won't make you any better, that's what you're going to take out - JUNK! I know you can think about this concept and use it to make you smarter and stronger.

This idea is something more powerful than money.

Your internal bank account is also under the influence of the people we meet. This is why it is important to choose the people we hang around - some will help you with deposits and others will take everything away in less than a minute.

Yesterday, we talked about habits and how they can either help us succeed or take us far away from our goal. You also identified the habits you want to pick up. These habits will improve your internal bank account balance, help you perform your daily tasks and create your wonderful future.

Make more deposits than withdrawals.

Keeping a daily tally of points on your scorecard helps you know if you're making progress in this CHALLENGE. This is important because when you realize that you're making progress, you're usually motivated to do more.

Your internal bank is filled with the things that motivate you. Many times, this is a reflection of your values and the things you enjoy. Be sure to deposit the right kind of habits in your internal bank every day so that when you need to make a withdrawal, you will have a large balance instead of that overdraft penalty and problems.

DAY 3 - MY INTERNAL BANK

Exercise #1 - Determine Your Internal Bank Balance

Today, we need to look at our internal bank account and how we can add to our future or hurt it with silly habits we might not even realize we have. Since habits can determine whether or not we meet our goals, it is best for us to pick up and nurture the right kinds of habits. We must recognize the ones that take us away from the results we want to see. That way, we intentionally shape our future.

It's time to think about it and make some decisions. What habits do you have in your internal bank? How many have you deposited today? How many bad habits have made you withdraw? Do very bad habits count extra? YES!! What is your balance?

Here is an example of how to take an accounting of your life and your daily balance.

Starting today = 0 Balance

Additions +1 for each = healthy food, sleep, friendship time, exercise, attendance = 5 Balance

Subtracting - 1 for each = anger, lying, skipping school = 2 Balance for the day

Look back at your list about your habits from yesterday. Calculate your balance using the guide above. Turn back to that page and actually do the calculations. Do you have a positive balance or are you overdrawn and broke?

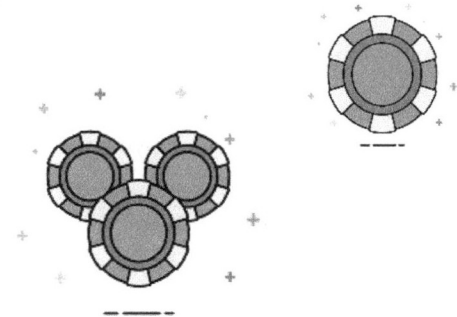

Exercise #2 - How To Make My Bank

The CHALLENGE scorecard is designed to help you focus on the positive behaviors that will make you successful in life. I want you to challenge yourself to earn every point and find ways to go above and beyond on SMART Tasks.

Working on this every day is guaranteed to make you smarter and keep you on track toward the future of your dreams. Be honest with yourself and pay attention to what you are doing, you will see amazing things happen. Think about the ways you can make deposits into your internal account. And, seriously, what has got to stop with those negative withdrawals?

I can increase my balance with _____

I will stop making these withdrawals _____

Your Daily Scorecard

1 Point for Each	Diet - Fitness - Water - Sleep - Attendance - Gratitude	
2 Points for Each	Attitude - Schoolwork - Warm-up Questions	Add It Up!
5 Points for Each	Daily Exercises	
10 Points	SMART Wakeup	
BONUS Points	SMART Tasks	

DEPOSIT TOTAL FOR TODAY

MY POINTS =

Coaching Tip From Ms. Peck –

Did you do the morning routine when you woke up this morning? I am going to keep you focused on good habits and practicing skills for a smarter start in life. Personally, music, yoga and lots of water is my way to start the day. Be aware of your good habits so your identity is not shaped by bad habits instead.

Equipment Room Alert

We have an appendix of resources or an "Equipment Room" at the end of the workbook to help you build on these ideas. Look at the end of the workbook today for more info about self-care.

Day 4 - Strengthen My Willpower

Warm-up Questions:

1. What challenges are you facing as a teen?
2. What problems have you faced in the past at school?
3. How do you approach your problems when you have one?
4. What's your attitude when you fail at something difficult?
5. What motivates you to tackle difficult situations?

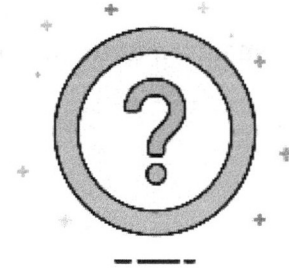

Power Words: Problem Solving, Internal Motivators, Resilience

Problem Solving: The process of finding solutions to difficult or complex issues.

Internal Motivators: The inner thoughts, feelings/emotions, values or reasoning that push us or inspire us to do something or achieve a goal.

Resilience: When a person uses mental processes and behaviors to promote or protect themselves from negative effects or problems.

Lesson:

When miners blast the Earth's crust or archaeologists dig up ancient ruins, they are searching for treasure. The treasure could be oil, dinosaurs or some important historical artifact. They spend days, weeks and even months in their hunt and get tired but they never stop working. At other times, they check their maps and look at the charts to be sure they are on the right trail. If they are certain that they are, they keep digging nonstop until they strike gold, or the payoff.

Determination is what fuels their consistency. Sometimes, they spend so long trying to do what everyone else thinks is impossible. They endure harsh weather conditions and have to eat food that doesn't taste too good. Sometimes, they have to stay in places where there is no electricity or water. But they don't quit because they're uncomfortable, they are following a process.

They keep on searching because they are motivated by the thrill of a new discovery or by the kind of wealth they would come by when they're successful. When things get rough, their internal motivator keeps them going. They see, feel and taste what success would bring for them. They know that if it's worth searching for, it's worth all the effort. They hold on to their no-quitter attitude, trust their process and achieve results.

Sometimes, they do fail. When that happens, they go over their goals, their strategies and they brainstorm for better ideas to try. Then, they can pinpoint why they failed, make some adjustments and start all over again. It is important to develop the ability to recover from a failure enough to look it straight in the eye and examine all the parts that made it happen. Critical thinking solves problems and prevents them from happening again.

We can learn from the treasure hunters' resilience and mental strength. Rather than run from our problems, we should face them headlong and tackle them. Rather than let those problems put you in a bad mood, think about solutions instead. Ask yourself: "How can I fix this? What do I need to learn or do to make this problem go away?"

With problem solving skills, you can use strategies and find solutions.

If your problem is having a failing grade in gym class, be honest and think, is it really because you dislike running in front of everybody on race day? Ask yourself: "How do I get myself to actually like this enough to participate and earn a decent grade"? What if you thought about a reward you could give yourself if you ran around your neighborhood for practice before the big race day? Who could you help with a quick run to a store?

When you change up how you look at the situation, or put yourself in a better mental location, you can get through a difficult situation with success. So instead of the track at school which stresses you out, what if you made a quick jog to the grocery store with your backpack to pick up a few things for your mom? The exercise would be good for you as a runner but more importantly, the reward or satisfaction of helping your family becomes your motivator.

And, you know, getting a good grade in gym (and every class) is always rewarded. So, you decide to get your shoes and go for that run and sure enough, all kinds of deposits are made into your internal bank. You are being smart to practice running and make those feelings or deposits today so you can use them tomorrow at school.

Day 4 - Strengthen My Willpower

Some experts call this re-framing the situation. When you are smart and stop to re-think, there's always a way to solve a problem. In every solution, there is a motivation or something the person wants to change, and that is their negative position into a positive one. In this situation, ask yourself what's in it for you to do something different and find the solution.

Back to our story about motivation. The next day, when you are standing at the race starting point, I know you will remember those family feelings and it will help you run with that smile. I also know you will make the time you need to show the gym teacher you can demonstrate that skill and get that grade.

So, ok I know that sounds easy, let's try it again.

What if you try several times at something and you're still not doing a good job? Don't let the feeling of failure overwhelm you. Instead, pause and ask yourself: "Why isn't this working out? What should I be doing differently?" Exhale and think. In order to answer these questions honestly, you'll have to take a step back and re-strategize. Maybe you set your goal too high or maybe your reward was not tempting enough.

When you re-frame the problem, you adjust how you look at the situation. It is not about finding blame; it is about taking ownership and being responsible for the situation. Thinking of your problems in this different way makes you get things done and changes you from being a whiner or a complainer to becoming a problem solver.

Sometimes, we have problems that we can't tackle on our own. Maybe you can't concentrate in class because you aren't seeing properly, and you need glasses. Or you have panic attacks and anxiety over a failed test, and you need to schedule a makeup test with a teacher. Perhaps, you're having trouble sleeping or difficulty getting your thoughts together and need to talk with a mental health counselor.

You cannot keep ignoring the problem hoping it will go away. Sometimes, people need to see a professional to resolve situations. It is really not a big deal. You may make the situation worse and hurt yourself more if you continue to ignore it.

Instead, I am telling you to speak up for yourself and seek help. You may need a doctor's visit for some medical advice. You may also need some medication or some psychological therapy. They also have support groups that make sure you're doing okay because lots of people have lots of different kinds of problems and finding solutions is a good thing to happen.

Exercise #1- Identifying The Problems

Before you solve a problem, you must know what it is and how it is pulling you down or preventing you from reaching your goal. In this exercise, you will think about the past school year and the setbacks or problems you've had in your life and in school.

Here are 4 questions that will help you analyze a difficult situation. Use this as an example and answer these questions for any problem or conflict you may have. Describe all the details as you can, this is time for critical thinking about your obstacles. Be honest and dig deeper to think about motivation and what someone really wants in order to solve the problem. Can you give advice to these students to help them with how to resolve their situation? Add your ideas or suggestions to this chart.

What is the problem?	Who else is involved?	What is the conflict really about?	What have you done in the situation?
Missing the bus and school	Bus driver	Waking up late, eating, dressing and lost backpack	Blame the bus driver for being early
Bad grade in math	Mr. Thompson, Dave and Joe	Mr. Thompson talks fast Dave and Joe talk to me	Laugh and talk with Dave and Joe
Gossip about me	Debbie and Alexis	Debbie's old boyfriend started walking me to class	Told another friend how mean and ugly Debbie is

DAY 4 - STRENGTHEN MY WILLPOWER

What is the problem(s)?	Who else is involved?	What is the conflict really about?	What have you done in the situation?

Exercise #2 - Separate The Problems You Can Tackle And Do It

Look through the list of problems you've written in the warm-up and honestly assess them one by one. Which ones do you have control over? Which ones can you tackle by motivating yourself with a great reward? What can you do to solve your own problems? Now, make it happen.

Which problems seem to happen almost against your will? Are problems because of how your mind is reacting or how your body is feeling? How can you change your diet or self-care habits to strengthen yourself and build up your resilience?

Which problems are just too much and scare you to death? Be honest with yourself and make some decisions to solve your problems. Sometimes, getting help from another person is the solution you need.

Being able to admit it, and say, "here is my problem and I want to work past it" is a giant accomplishment. When you are using your brain and willpower to make good decisions, your future can only be successful.

Use these sentence starters to analyze each problem and look for motivations within yourself and the other people involved.

- The problems I have control over are:
- The problems I can tackle by motivating myself are:
- The problems I may need help for are:
- The internal motivators that would help me build up my resilience are:

Life is full of choices and you hold the power of how your life goes. If you can think of problems as mistakes and things to learn along the way, you are being smarter. You should not be afraid of making a mistake, Thomas Edison said he made thousands of mistakes before he made the light bulb.

Strengthen your willpower to keep looking for solutions to your problems. Adopt a "Never Give Up" attitude. Those bad situations are just roadblocks you can get past with some thinking!

Your Scorecard For Today

1 Point for Each	Diet - Fitness - Water - Sleep - Attendance - Gratitude	
2 Points for Each	Attitude - Schoolwork - Warm-up Questions	**Add It Up!**
5 Points for Each	Daily Exercises	
10 Points	SMART Wakeup	
BONUS Points	SMART Tasks	

DEPOSIT TOTAL FOR TODAY

MY POINTS =

Coaching Tip From Ms. Peck -

The best way to keep doing your Smart Start Wakeup every morning, is to set your alarm clock with a special ringtone. Your brain is a muscle that needs working out and any little tip that works, do it. Memories are like ripples; they have energy and need a boost sometimes. Don't get frustrated when you practice critical thinking – you're building up resilience to conquer the world!

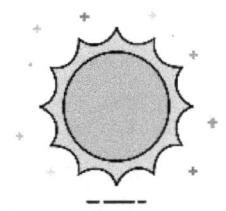

Equipment Room Alert - There is another problem-solving organizer for you to use, it can help you identify the details often hidden within a conflict. If you get stuck in a tough situation, look at the back of the handbook for more resources. Remember, problem solving is a process and this tool or strategy works.

Day 5 - All-Star School Plan

Warm-up Questions:

1. What is your toughest challenge at school and why does this happen?
2. Have you considered getting a tutor?
3. Do you know how to get help during class when you need it?
4. Are there ways or certain times when learning is easy for you?
5. Do your parents/guardians reward your efforts shown by your report card?

Power Words: Intelligence, Learning Styles

Intelligence: The ability to learn or understand things or to deal with new or difficult situations.

Learning Styles: A well regarded theory explains how people will think differently when they learn. People use many ways to gather, interpret, organize, evaluate, reach conclusions and "store" information for further use.

Lesson:

I have heard from students that they think school is just some place they have to go to learn a bunch of boring stuff. They say, it is a waste of time and they do not learn anything that really helps them in their future. When I hear that, my heart just breaks. If this is true for you, I am sorry for your bad experience, and I am so happy you are here with me now!

If you are struggling at school, your attitude to school and learning will be negative. I get it, bad experiences mean bad things, but please give me a chance to help you change that around. When the reason for schooling is unclear, many students shut down in failure or act out for attention. It does not have to be that way and this SMART START CHALLENGE is going to strengthen you and get you past whatever hurdle is holding you back.

First, school is not a place we have to go.

It's a place we get to go and learn about things that will help us in the career paths we have chosen. At school (or with online distance learning), we learn things that prepare us to be responsible adults in the world. Millions of children around the world do not have access to a free education. It is a great opportunity to go to school and it is not something you should ever miss out on because of some bad experiences.

In school, we learn how to communicate our thoughts clearly in our speech and in our writing, and these are critical skills when job hunting. We should learn to appreciate our history, so we stop repeating the same mistakes. We also need to learn about scientific discoveries and technological innovations to inspire us to want to invent something too. Unfortunately, too many students are not having this type of experience.

Remember our discussion about attitude and how you frame, or re-frame a situation? A person can shift their perspective of things. This is a perfect example of that happening. What if you reconsidered your education?

Seriously, consider these points. Our imagination is energized when we read fiction from creative writers like Mark Twain, J.D. Salinger or Harper Lee. Learning about revolutionary thinkers like Leonardo da Vinci, Galileo or Albert Einstein truly has an impact today, as we explore space and begin to create artificial intelligence.

We can also learn about activists – the heroes and heroines, who risked their lives and their freedom to speak for building a country of laws and justice. In America, George Washington, Abigale Adams and Alexander Hamilton are just the beginning of our story. Today, we enjoy the things they fought for and tomorrow you can be protesting to shape the laws of the future. In school, we are intrigued by many true stories and we can be inspired to live for something bigger than ourselves.

If you see your courses this new way, you will connect with them. Connecting with them makes them relatable and makes you appreciate and understand them better. If we change the negative attitude, maybe we can see the good things at school.

I know not every teacher is as fabulous as me, but, no truthfully, most of them are. Being a teacher is difficult because we are trained on all these great evidence-based methods for teaching, but then every student is different. I am asking you to give your teachers a break and take responsibility for YOU getting YOUR education. I need you to step back from your hurt feelings and think about school from another viewpoint.

At this point, you need to realize the game is not going to change. The reality of classes, teachers, homework and grades is what it is. One school is pretty much like the next one. The only thing you can change is YOUR ATTITUDE about it.

So, here's the cool, insider part that you are learning in the SMART START CHALLENGE...

Everyone learns differently and when you learn in your "style" you will learn quickly and easily. When you match how you learn with the information you need to learn, there is no stopping you!

Psychologist and education researcher, Howard Gardner, developed a theory called Multiple Intelligences in 1982. Simply put, people learn things in different ways and all of the styles are considered "intelligence". Students need to use the style that matches how their brain works and teachers need to teach in many different styles.

To Gardner, grades aren't a true test of knowledge. Usually, schools tend to box people together and ask students to memorize or learn things a certain way. This old-fashioned approach to education does not work for everyone and you need to make the adjustment to learn the way that works best for you.

Some people can see and think in numbers while others need to hear stories. Some people learn from being hands on; that's the only way they understand and relate to concepts. Some others prefer videos or pictures. There are some people who have natural aptitude for language. Some are great with music or must be in nature.

Every type or form of intelligence is valid. And although schools today are a lot better than before, I know that sometimes you feel left out or lost during classes. Now that you know about these different ways of learning, you are going to identify which ones work best for you. When you are engaged in learning YOUR style, YOU will be excited to learn.

If you have stinking thoughts and believe you are stupid or too dumb to learn, STOP IT! Intelligence is not about HOW smart you are, it is about HOW YOU are smart. Today, you are going to decide what works best for you and tomorrow you are going to decide how to use your learning style in your classes. Everything is changing because you are in this SMART START CHALLENGE and working toward your fabulous future!

Exercise #1 - Check-in With School

Today, we talked about your grades and how your attitude impacts your ability to get your education. While getting good grades is important, fully understanding the information is the goal. In this exercise, you're going to examine your current academic situation. You are also going to look at your grades and consider the steps you need to take to ensure you graduate.

Compare your grades to this student. Change the grades and comments to reflect your current status at school. Just cross out the teachers names and change the grades and situation in the space below. Add as necessary and use this chart as a guide.

Class#	Course	Teacher	Grade	Situation
1	English	Jones	D	Old teacher and 7am time
2	Reading	Davis	D	I have to take this until I meet graduation
3	Gym	Webber	A	I love sports of course
4	Art	Adams	A	It is creative, I get to choose what I do
5	Math	Thompson	D	He talks fast and my friends talk to me
6	Science	Dupont	C	Fun but too much homework
7	History	West	C	BORING and worksheets I can copy

DAY 5 - ALL-STAR SCHOOL PLAN

Recognize your strengths and abilities in the classes you are doing well in. Then, identify the subjects or teachers that cause you to struggle, consider what the difference is between these two types of situations. Being honest with yourself is about taking responsibility - never blame, just think about it and correct it to improve it!

You take the first step in the problem-solving process when you start to analyze the situation. This student must change how they are getting their education because it looks pretty bad to me. This is not about criticism; it is about making a change for the better. When you do this analysis, be honest and try and dig deeper into the real issues because that is where you will find the solutions.

You also know that a certain grade point average is required for graduation. As you continue from middle to high school, those classes with "C" grades start pulling your future down. The more C's you have, the more A's you need to balance it out. When you understand how to use your style of learning, you will have that SMART START at school. Graduation may seem years away, but it is not!

Exercise # 2 - Find My Learning Style

Earlier, we saw that people learn things differently. Some people remember stories while some love pictures and others love numbers. Howard Gardner was the first to recognize that there are lots of ways to be "intelligent" and that knowing which type you are helps you be successful in school.

As you read each description, take notes about how you use each of these types of learning. Put a check mark by the ones you feel comfortable using.

Verbal-linguistic	**Well-developed verbal skills and sensitivity to the sounds, meanings and rhythms of words**
Logical-mathematical	**Ability to think conceptually and abstractly, and capacity to discern logical and numerical patterns**
Spatial-visual	**Capacity to think in images and pictures, to visualize accurately and abstractly**

Bodily-kinesthetic	Ability to control one's body movements and to handle objects skillfully
Musical	Ability to produce and appreciate rhythm, pitch and timber
Interpersonal	Capacity to detect and respond appropriately to the moods, motivations and desires of others
Intrapersonal	Capacity to be self-aware and in tune with inner feelings, values, beliefs and thinking processes
Naturalist	Ability to recognize and categorize plants, animals and other objects in nature
Existential	Sensitivity and capacity to tackle deep questions about human existence such as, "What is the meaning of life? Why do we die? How did we get here?"

Consider how you enjoy learning new things and what sparks your brain into warp speed. When are you "in your groove" and time flies by because you love working on your kind of project?

For example, if a student loved nature and being outdoors, it would make sense to go study outside, or look at your science book and find an experiment to do on your own using things found in nature. When you do this, you are learning in your style. Go do it.

- Pick two or three types of learning that suit you best.
- How can you use your favorite learning style in one of those difficult classes you have?
- Which teacher(s) can you speak with about using your learning style in assignments?

Exercise #3 - Talking With Parents Or Guardians

I need you to consider what your family wants from you. Think about what you can do to improve the situation and then do it because the reward is guaranteed. If they want better grades, writing every day will demonstrate that you are working to bring up that English class grade.

The final part of today's lesson is for you to talk to your parents or guardians about rewarding your efforts in this SMART START CHALLENGE. You learned about internal motivations and those feelings you get when you do something right. Now, I want you to think about those external motivators or rewards that also drive you to action.

If you make a few notes about what you are doing differently this month and reasons why you deserve a reward, it will help you when you are talking face to face. You could make it in two parts; something for completing the CHALLENGE and something bigger for a great final tally on the scorecard (1,850 points are possible!).

The reward doesn't have to be something expensive – just something special that will motivate you every day. Maybe your favorite dinner or a new baseball cap in only 26 short days would remind you how important it is to work every day for your success.

External motivators are things outside of you that are incentives to entice you into action. When you have a job, you get a paycheck. Same thing is applicable in your personal life. If you want a new baseball cap and will go practice to build up your skills to hit it out of the park on game day, that's an external motivator. Sure, the cheers are great, but you want that cap to wear to school or the movies.

I want you to understand that you are also working on improving your relationship with and within yourself, and with your family. You are discovering more about yourself and what really matters to you. Talking about the CHALLENGE and sharing the good and bad, always strengthens you and helps you in life.

What kind of external reward would motivate you to work hard at your goal?

Negotiate with your family and make a deal for your SMART START CHALLENGE reward!

Write yours out: My external motivators are _____

My reward for completing the SSC and earning over _____ points will be _____

Today's Scorecard

1 Point for Each	Diet - Fitness - Water - Sleep - Attendance - Gratitude	
2 Points for Each	Attitude - Schoolwork - Warm-up Questions	**Add It Up!**
5 Points for Each	Daily Exercises	
10 Points	SMART Wakeup	
BONUS Points	SMART Tasks	

DEPOSIT TOTAL FOR TODAY

MY POINTS =

Coaching Tip From Ms. Peck –

Here is a reminder to keep your overall points current on the Track Your Stats Report on pages 20-21. It is important to evaluate your written responses against the expectations shown in the student samples. Add up how many details you have written or examples you used. If you are not meeting the writing requirement here, you will not be able to meet it for graduation and that is a big problem. Practice at 100% to earn 100%.

You are practicing critical thinking and learning how to use new skills. I hope you are challenging yourself during this SMART START CHALLENGE. Are you beginning to feel smarter already? Tomorrow is another big day - be sure you are at your best and get plenty of sleep tonight!

Day 6 - All-Star Student Setup

Warm-up Questions:

1. Do you use an academic planner?
2. Do you have a specific home study area?
3. Do you turn in your schoolwork on time?
4. What time do you work on your homework?
5. Do you have problems with meeting deadlines?

Power Words: Time Management, Study Area

Time Management: The ability to use one's time effectively or productively. Time management is also the process of organizing and planning how to divide your time between your activities.

Study Area: A space in your home specifically for study where you have everything you need to practice and learn.

Lesson:

One key ingredient to success is cultivating and practicing the right kind of habits. We have seen that habits predict who you are going to eventually become. One of the habits to pick up is Time Management. If you don't seem to get things done on time, you should take a step back and reflect on this topic and fix it.

Sometimes, it could be because you're spending too much time on the wrong things and are rushing through what you need to do with the little time you have left. Doing as little as possible is not being on the road to success. Treating your schoolwork that way will never take you where you want to go in life. It makes you turn in poor work which earns you terrible grades. And, when you turn in poorly done work, you don't understand the assignment as a foundation for what then needs to build upon that information. If you cannot do addition, then multiplication is impossible.

Yesterday, we saw that school isn't just a place we are made to go. We saw that the things we learn at school help shape who we become; they put us on the right career path and help us achieve our dreams. When we fully understand how important this is, we would treat our schoolwork with respect. That way, we would put the most into it to get the most out of it.

You need to understand that your schoolwork is actually the most important thing to you right now. So, you should treat it like it matters a lot more than everything else, because it really does. You should tackle homework right away, so you can go on to do fun things when it is done and you feel great about it. Schoolwork isn't always fun, that's why it's called work.

Prioritize and put first things first.

The interesting thing about schoolwork is that you only get results matching the kind of efforts you put in. Simply put, what you see is what you get. If you show up anytime you like, skip classes whenever you feel like and study only whenever you choose, chances are that your grades are just as poor as your attitude.

I know school has been tough lately, but that is why we are going through this right here and now. You must decide to give it your best shot, like the miners we talked about, keep working until you get good results!

Exercise #1 - All-Star Student Success Survey

Answer the following questions honestly about your current attitude or work practices toward school. Some answers are better than others and I hope you can see how each action you take has an effect. I hope you will see the connection between those good and bad habits and how they can hurt you at school.

Focus:

Do you feel you are eating the proper diet? Yes _____ No _____

Do you feel that you get enough sleep at night to be successful in school? Yes _____ No _____

Are you easily distracted or catch yourself daydreaming? Yes _____ No _____

Do you turn off the television or music when you do homework? Yes _____ No _____

Do you exercise or spend more than 30 minutes a day being active? Yes _____ No _____

Day 6 - All-Star Student Setup

Self-Control:

Are you aware that organization skills are needed throughout our lives? Yes _____ No _____

Do you know that setting goals for yourself helps you stay on track with life? Yes _____ No _____

Are you able to ignore distractions when they arise in class? Yes _____ No _____

Do you have rules at home with punishment or consequences if broken? Yes _____ No _____

Do you hold yourself accountable for the actions that you are responsible for? Yes _____ No _____

Self-Confidence:

Do you often say you can't or don't know how to do your homework? Yes _____ No _____

Do you feel safe and secure at school? Yes _____ No _____

Do you take pride in your clothing and appearance? Yes _____ No _____

Do you ask for help, or tutoring when you don't understand something? Yes _____ No _____

Are you willing to try new things or take risks? Yes _____ No _____

Study Skills:

Do you have enough time after school to work on homework assignments? Yes _____ No _____

Do you prioritize your work? (Most important or earliest deadline first) Yes _____ No _____

Do you complete your homework before you enjoy free time? Yes _____ No _____

When you do homework:

Do you have somewhere quiet to work? Yes _____ No _____

Do you sit at a table or desk instead of lying on the floor or bed? Yes _____ No _____

Do you have all the supplies you need to complete it? Yes _____ No _____

Do you use your agenda to keep track of assignments and due dates? Yes _____ No _____

Exercise #2 - Finding A Tutor Or Other Resources

If you look at your answers from the survey, you will probably see the areas that need help. When you take the time now to consider where you can step up, you can also identify the areas you need help with. It is time to speak up.

If you're having difficulty with your classes in school, you should speak with your teacher immediately. Getting the information about what you need to study, can only come from the person who is teaching and grading you. You can write a note if you don't want to speak in front of your friends.

The next step is to find someone who could re-teach you or help you practice. You may need a tutor – someone to help you break down the concepts in ways you can relate with or understand.

There are lots of other resources at school that can help you if you are having personal issues that are getting in the way of school. My school has career guidance counselors, social workers, day care, job placement and even a foodbank and laundry.

As a student, you have lots of help available but only when you ask for it. Asking for help just means you are smart enough to know you need help. Look at that All-Star Student survey and notes about your grades, what kind of help do you need to go find? Go do it.

Exercise #3 - Setting Up My Home Study Area - SMART Task

Finally, for this SMART Task, you are going to set-up a personal work area. An All-Star Student needs a quiet space just for studying. You need to set up a table and chair along with your computer or notebooks. Imagine that I am coming over to see it, you know it needs to be clean and organized. You need to create a space for your genius to be happy.

We have talked about how important it is to take your schoolwork seriously. Here are a few tips to help you create a great study area:

- The area should have good lighting and ventilation.
- It should be as far away as possible from your bed.
- It shouldn't be near the kitchen either.
- It should be somewhere private (and quiet).
- It should be organized and clean.
- You should have your planner stuck right above where your eyes can see it.
- It shouldn't be too comfortable.
- There should be lots of space especially on the table.
- No TV, phones or gadgets should be allowed in the study area.
- Keep all your study materials close.
- Your study area should only be used for studying.

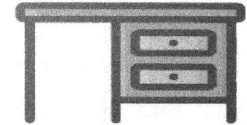

Next, you need to create a planner of some sort, if you do not have one already. Time management is another thing you need to learn how to do. It is easy to start using the calendar in your phone or in your email account. All-Stars schedule time to study for each class and make sure they turn in every assignment on time. Seriously, why give away points for a bad timing habit?

I mentioned it before, but setting alarms is a genius move. Your alarms can remind you when it's time to start studying and when it's time to run for the morning bus. Name them and give them different ring tones. It is fun to hear cheers for the dinner break alarm!

Ok, things to do today for the SMART Task

- Organize a study area.
- Get a planner and start using it.
- Set your alarms to make your morning routine happen easily.

You were so smart to get everything you need for success setup in one place. It should energize you and feel like it's "my workspace". Being prepared for the best things ahead is another way you are getting smarter every day!

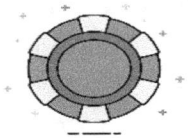

Congratulations, you are almost done with the first week of the SMART START CHALLENGE!!

Today's Scorecard

1 Point for Each	Diet - Fitness - Water - Sleep - Attendance - Gratitude	
2 Points for Each	Attitude - Schoolwork - Warm-up Questions	**Add It Up!**
5 Points for Each	Daily Exercises	
10 Points	SMART Wakeup	*DEPOSIT TOTAL FOR TODAY*
BONUS Points	SMART Tasks	*MY POINTS =*

SMART Task Bonus Points +25 for All-Star Setup

Coaching Tip From Ms. Peck –

Researchers have determined that our brain power is like a machine of processes needed to carry out any task. Being smart is about how you learn, how you remember and pay attention to important things. Being smart is not just the facts and knowledge you learn from books or teachers. Thinking also includes your perception or what you think about things and the words you use to explain the world around you.

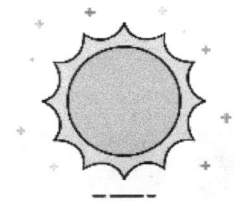

I hope you feel stronger now that you are taking control of your future. It takes a little bit each day and it starts to build up and get powerful. I know your brain training is starting to work. You are almost done with Round #1 of Coaching, it might be early, but are you feeling the new energy?

Day 7 - Catalyst For Change

Warm-up Questions:

1. Have you ever done a WebQuest or internet research? When and why?
2. How do you search online safely?
3. Do you make short videos or post on social media? Explain
4. Have you ever consider how life could be in a foreign country?
5. What social issue do you think needs to change in your community? Why?

Power Words: Brainstorm, Catalyst, WebQuest

Brainstorm: A thinking activity where you try to come up with many new ideas. It is important to think in lots of creative ways and to never judge an idea while brainstorming.

Catalyst: A person or thing that starts an action - a spark creates a flame is an example.

WebQuest: A WebQuest is an inquiry-oriented process or research activity where the information you seek comes from the internet and a variety of websites.

Lesson:

Social issues are problems that affect a large number of people around us and in our community. As a young person, learning about the things that affect our society helps shape your views on these important issues. It also helps you become empathetic, or caring toward struggling people and maybe even a passion for doing something to fix it.

There are so many issues - it could be anything ranging from bullying, homelessness, alcohol or drug abuse, racism, sexism, poverty to pregnancy, HIV/AIDS, gun violence, mental health challenges, human trafficking and so on. Each of these problems affects millions of people all over the world. Sadly, a good number of teens are affected too.

This part of the CHALLENGE is very important for your growth and may help you find ways to deal with issues you are facing. It also helps you recognize the moral compass of any social movements or political party you choose to support, whether now or in the future.

To become more aware about the world around you, this is the beginning of your social project in which you explore our virtual planet and learn something about yourself. Thanks to the internet and social media, we can connect with people from different countries very easily. I want you to set up an inquiry and find teens around the world willing to share their story.

During this CHALLENGE, you are going to be conducting research and finding out how other parts of the world handle the same problems we face. This week, you need to brainstorm ideas for your project and decide which social issue you want to work on. You are going to identify the topic and begin searching for 3 teens in other countries.

Being a Catalyst for Change means doing something to make the world a better place.

A catalyst is a person or thing that makes something else happen. During this CHALLENGE, you are going to create something to drive social change for an issue you feel is important. The project is a way to strengthen your ability to communicate clearly – in your speech and in writing.

I will give you more specific requirements later, but for now, I can tell you the final project is to make a one-minute video that you can post on our websites - SmartStartChallenge.com and AskMsPeck.com and on your social media.

Don't worry about the video, that will be easy. For now, think and decide WHAT social issue you are passionate about. What issue has gotten deep into your core – perhaps because you have experienced it, or you know someone who has? Or perhaps you just hate the thought of it, and you wish it will go away.

Fighting social issues is not as easy as it sounds. Sometimes, it takes years, decades, even centuries, but the change made may be barely visible. This shouldn't make us slow down or give up. Rather, we should add fuel to fire and intensify our efforts in fighting for what we believe.

DAY 7 - CATALYST FOR CHANGE

Exercise #1 - Developing Your Belief System

Your belief system is the set of things you value or take seriously. It could be virtues we talked about on Day 1: wisdom, honesty, independence, natural, fun and so on. Our belief system affects what we do and how we do it. Beliefs or values also influence the way we treat other people.

Our belief system, if we believe the right kind of things, helps us empathize with others when they're not being treated fairly. Part of growing up is choosing your belief system. You get to decide the kind of adult you want the world to see. You are in this SMART START CHALLENGE to learn how to take charge of your life.

So, think about the social issues that get your blood boiling. It could be something you have personally dealt with or something you can only imagine and think about how hurtful it must be. The exercises today include you making a decision about which cause/issue you are going to be working for. Pick something that aligns or matches your values or beliefs.

We began the challenge with your personal mission statement, and I want you to look back on that and consider this list below. Do you need to adjust what you were thinking a few days ago, or maybe add to the values you hold most dear?

Pick a social issue and write down your first ideas about why this issue must change. Explain what it means to you and what makes it so wrong. Brainstorm to think up lots of reasons why we must fix the problem.

As you begin doing the research on your social issue, look for examples of these values in the lives of teens, just like you. Be sure to capture your ideas on paper (or digitally on your computer). When you take notes, every idea is important, and you will want lots of them when you begin turning your research into your video presentation.

Use this list as a vocabulary cheat-sheet. I want to help you get started putting down details and reasoning in your writing. What makes you tick - circle it!

Encouragement	**Humor**	**Leadership**	**Friendship**	**Justice**	**Finances**
Knowledge	**Compassion**	**Balance**	**Courage**	**Entertainment**	**Personality**
Home	**Relationship**	**Being true**	**Change**	**Career**	**Fitness**

Humanity	Freedom	Religion	Order	Beauty	Innovation
Openness	Diversity	Respect	Advancement	Patience	Cooperation
Joy/Play	Fairness	Faith	Goodness	Friendship(s)	Endurance
Creativity	Wisdom	Invention	Involvement	Security	Grace
Power	Excitement	Generosity	Adventure	Fame	Wellness
Integrity	Teamwork	Love	Change	Willingness	Gratitude
Intelligence	Learning	Caring	Strength	Happiness	Curiosity
Kindness	Forgiveness	Honesty	Appreciation	Self-Respect	Community
Quality	Affection	Excellence	Enjoyment	Peace	Hope

Write down your thoughts about your choice of issue to promote as a Catalyst for Change. Why is this important to you?

Exercise #2 - Begin A Social Issue WebQuest

Create an internet search for the issue you have decided to work on for this project. You need to find 3 young adults (or under 25 years old) from other countries that are facing the same social issue.

As you dig deeper in your virtual world, look for 3 young people who are involved with activism in their community. Look for news stories or non-profit organizations. Social media is ok but go visit their websites too. Search by different countries and the topic, switch it up.

I hope by now you know how to surf the web safely. Be sure you stay on websites that are credible and reliable. News and nonprofit organizations are the best places to start looking. Blogs or social media are ok if they are written by someone under 25 years old. Those independent authors will have a first-person viewpoint which can be very powerful. Take note of the domain addresses you visit so you can make a bibliography when you are finished.

This first research WebQuest should be done over several days and I know you will find several young people doing amazing things. You do not have to contact them, just remember, safety online is a Ms. Peck requirement. This is the beginning of the final project due on Day #29, you are using an inquiry-research process and will be guided along the way.

This might be a good time to expand your note taking, there's space at the end of the Handbook. You can create a list of information for each person you find. Here's a few questions to get you started but I want you to brainstorm your own in this space. The researched answers can be short; you're just getting started in the process - smarter!

The social issue I am interested in: **BRAINSTORM MORE QUESTIONS:**

The people I connected with are _____ in _____ country:

- **How does the social issue affect them?**

- **Who/What is their major cause or reason for the problem?**

- **What are they doing to help?**

Exercise #3 - Social Issue Discussion - SMART Task

Sometimes, you have 3 exercises to really build up your muscles. And, this one build upon Day #5, Exercise #3. Once you have decided on your social issue and begun some research, I want you to discuss the project with your family. Working on this project during the CHALLENGE is a big deal and takes both internal and external motivation and rewards. I want you to continue discussing the Catalyst project with friends too. Sharing your research helps you think about it and validate your ideas.

Explain how your family reacted to your selection of a social issue and their general thoughts about the project.

Today's Scorecard –

1 Point for Each	Diet - Fitness - Water - Sleep - Attendance - Gratitude	
2 Points for Each	Attitude - Schoolwork - Warm-up Questions	**Add It Up!**
5 Points for Each	Daily Exercises	
10 Points	SMART Wakeup	
BONUS Points	SMART Tasks	

DEPOSIT TOTAL FOR TODAY

MY POINTS =

SMART Task Bonus 25+ Social Issue Discussion

Coaching Tip From Ms. Peck –

☑ *It is a good idea to gather a little information every day for this Catalyst for Change Project. Today's exercises should feel like a virtual field trip going around the world in search of teens facing similar issues. If you find something interesting, dig a little deeper and explore to find even more new ideas.*

You have completed the first week of the CHALLENGE, so be sure your stats are current because you should have a "Green Light" to go to the next round – yea!

Day 8 - Having A Global Vision

Warm-up Questions:

1. What have you learned in the past week?
2. What is your favorite learning style? Why?
3. How do you cope with difficult situations?
4. Which social issue did you decide to research and why?
5. Why is it important to understand things that caused, or led to social issues?

Power Words: External Motivators, Social Issue

External Motivators: These are external rewards like money, fame, grades and praise that motivate you to accomplish something, complete a task or achieve a goal.

Social Issue: A social issue is a problem that affects many people within a society or community.

Lesson:

Now that you are a week into the CHALLENGE, I'm sure you are starting to get the routine of each day's work out. I hope you have decided that it is up to you to take charge of your life. You are learning new ways to handle life's ups and downs.

During the first week of the CHALLENGE, I'm sure you started to figure out what makes you unique. Everybody is different and deserves to be happy with life. Getting on the right path for YOU is the goal.

If you have been stressed, frustrated or unhappy, I hope this week has opened your mind to a better tomorrow. You don't have to run or hide from anyone. Rather, you should crawl out of your shell and work with me to get passed that roadblock. I am a coach to help you move forward toward your best future. Trust me and do what I am asking because it is to show you a way of reaching your dreams.

Many times, it's good to find out why you fell into a bad habit or why things started happening the way they did. Maybe you were upset about your dad or mum leaving. Or you wanted to fit in with the popular kids. Maybe you needed someone to talk to.

There is NO SHAME in any of this or in having moments of deep reflection about your life. Whatever it was that sent you on a downward spiral, you need to figure it out and make a breakaway from it. Identifying it, or calling it out, is the way to make it change into something better. It takes nerve to be honest with yourself. I know it is hard but it must be done.

This is why it's important to know the things that motivate you. Your internal and external motivators are going to help you get over your hurdles. You also need a lot of information too. Since you know that you want to be successful, you have to ask yourself, "If I continue down this road, would I get to the destination I desire?"

Remember that on Day 1, we talked about finding your direction. We saw that where you want to go has to match what you choose to do, otherwise you could end up in the wrong location.

On Day 2, we talked about choosing the right kind of habits because that way, you can make your dreams come true. When you think about the fact that your actions have consequences, it's easier to choose better. As a person who is smart and willing to live better, you should choose good habits over bad ones.

We also talked about our internal bank and how what we put into our minds is what we are going to get out of it. Hopefully, you have been saying your SMART START Wakeup and scoring your practice of daily self-care. Keeping your mind focused includes your body and working on your goals every day.

We also looked at how to solve problems by digging into them instead of ignoring them. Another thing you did was to check in on those grades and how you "work" at school. We learned about time management and you were able to start an amazing WebQuest that even took you around the world!

Awesome job doing all this thinking and brain training!

Exercise #1 - Making Global Connections

It is a giant world and you are starting to explore it. While you are still in the beginning stage of research, I want you to start making the connections between the social issue and what makes it such a big problem. Before you jump deep into your research and compare and contrast the situation in different countries, I want you to review the reasons you have as to why it is an important issue for you.

President John F. Kennedy said, "One person can make a difference, and everyone should try". I believe that and it motivates me every day to create and host this CHALLENGE.

I believe the world is an amazing place and when you learn more about it, you will learn more about yourself. I know I did in the 50+ countries I have visited. Since we live in a global community, it is important for YOU to know about it and decide what YOU think about it.

The world can be organized or divided into continents as most people agree upon. While borders of countries can change, the land masses are natural ways to discuss parts of the world. Throughout history, man has always explored and wanted to learn from new people and places. It used to take months to sail across the Atlantic Ocean but today, we can see people and places instantly on our phones and computers.

Today, I want you to think about the world and write down the countries you know, or the issues you know exist in other parts of the world. Brainstorm what you already know about famous people or popular destinations or recent news events.

Use this list of continents to spark your memory and flow of ideas. Fill this space with things you already know to get a SMART START on your Catalyst for Change project.

North America

Central America/Caribbean

South America

Europe

Africa

Asia

Oceania/Australia

Antarctica

Exercise #2 Endurance Training

In just one week, you have already done a lot of thinking and personal reflection and you're now making your way to your dream future. I would like you to share any two new, major ideas you've learned so far. Explain how you think they are helping you become a better person and improve in your schoolwork.

Review this list of topics and pick the two days with the greatest impact on you. For the exercise, write a paragraph for your two days including a description, an example and your explanation about why you selected it as a highlight of the week. Jot down a few notes here to get your brain activated.

1. Finding Direction
2. Get A Growth Mindset
3. My Internal Bank
4. Strengthen My Willpower
5. Allstar School Plan
6. Allstar Student Setup
7. Catalyst For Change
8. Having A Global Vision

STUDENT SAMPLE TARGET: "One of the most important topics for me this week was about my willpower. I learned about explorers and how they have to adjust and keep looking if they want the treasure. That is a good reminder for me because I give up really easily. If things do not go my way, I'm the first one to give it up and pretend I don't care. Truth is, I do care and I need to get a grip on that bad habit. Another topic I liked was that if I get myself organized and setup BEFORE I start working on a project, it is like a head-start. I feel that way when I am at football practice and all my equipment is ready to put on and play. I am usually the first one out on the field and that does give me a head-start against the competition. Two highlights this week and I am ready for more next week".

DAY 8 - HAVING A GLOBAL VISION

This is your first draft of a summary paragraph about the CHALLENGE. Use this space and follow the student sample but add your experiences and ideas. Giving examples will increase your scoring.

Which 2 days have had the greatest impact on your thinking and why?

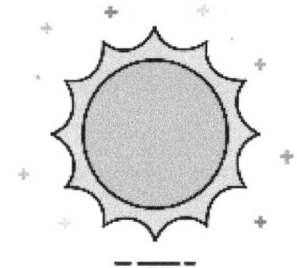

Today's Scorecard

Coaching Round #1 (Days 1-7) is over so you earned the weekly bonus 25+ points today!

1 Point for Each	Diet - Fitness - Water - Sleep - Attendance - Gratitude	
2 Points for Each	Attitude - Schoolwork - Warm-up Questions	Add It Up!
5 Points for Each	Daily Exercises	
10 Points	SMART Wakeup	
BONUS Points	SMART Tasks	

DEPOSIT TOTAL FOR TODAY

MY POINTS =

How will you CHALLENGE yourself to beat the first round score this next week?!

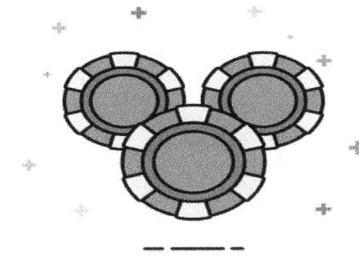

Coaching Tip From Ms. Peck –

I want you to remember these types of self-reflection activities are NEVER about blame or punishment. Being able to look at a situation and find ways to improve it for the next time it happens, is a life changing skill. Being honest with yourself is the only way it works. It does take a little bit of humility to say, "Ok, what could I do differently next time?"

And yes, this is part of learning to be accountable for controlling yourself and the freedoms you get with growing up. Responsibility can be defined as the opportunity to act independently and make decisions without authorization.

You are the one in charge of your future and being able to reflect on life helps you focus on where you are heading. The point is to learn from your experiences and do not repeat the negative stuff!!

Day 9 - Attitude Is Everything

Warm-up Questions:

1. How is your outlook on life and teenagerhood changing?

2. What are your expectations for school this year?

3. What beliefs spur you on to achieving great things?

4. What kind of negative thoughts or stinking thinking do you have?

5. What attitudes can help you get past difficult times?

Power Words: Attitude, Expectations

Attitude: The way you think and feel about someone or something.

Expectations: A belief that something will happen or is likely to happen.

Lesson:

Your attitude is the way you feel about life, the things you want to do, or not. Your attitude is your point of view that could spur you on to achieving great things. It can also be a huge weight that slows you down or stops you from reaching your goal. In other words, your attitude determines what you expect out of life. How you see things affects how far you are willing to go to make something happen.

When you don't expect to be successful, you won't put in a lot of work at school. You also won't be concerned about choosing healthy and productive habits or about how badly your grades are.

You create your point of view, or perspective of the world. What is your overall attitude?

Your attitude is a force that drives you more than anything external can. With the right attitude, you'd always be excited to get out of bed every day and get started on your morning routine. It is important to choose your attitudes carefully. Yes, it is a choice to have a good attitude because it affects how you work, the choices you make, what you choose to focus on and the opportunities that come to you.

Life isn't perfect. We have great times. But we go through tough times sometimes. We face difficult situations and sometimes, things don't always go the way we plan. How you process these situations, and the feelings you choose to keep when you are going through rough times, determines how well you'll do in your life and in your career.

If you decide to be all whiny and complain about every single thing that happens, you are more likely to be unsuccessful in the future. If you decide to feel bad or try to play the blame game, you will never win at what you want. This is because, rather than brainstorming or trying to find solutions, you'd be so focused on how terrible things are.

That's not a healthy attitude to have. When things get tough, the best thing is to get tough too and deal with it. Norman Vincent Peale said, "Change your thoughts and change your world." His book, *The Power of Positive Thinking*, was translated into 42 languages and has sold over 15 million copies since it was published in 1952.

I have my own way of saying it. When you choose to stop complaining or feeling low about everything, it's easier to think clearly and find solutions. Positive energy or thoughts have to create positive solutions. It's also easier to keep hope alive and simply wait out the tide if you can't change the situation.

Control your thoughts, control your future.

As a teen, this is the time to choose to be positive and to start thinking thoughts that make you want to put in work for things to be the way YOU want. It's also time to stop looking for who to blame for things that go wrong. Rather, choose to think about how to solve problems and prevent them from happening again.

Some great attitudes to pick up are the "Peak Performance" and "No-Quitter" types of strong willpower. When you are focused on giving your best performance, there's no room for second best. You should always want to put in maximum efforts and be the very best you can. So, you push yourself further every day and you will seek to improve upon yesterday's work.

A "No-Quitter" attitude builds grit and tenacity. It helps you to keep working even when it seems like you're not making headway. Like the miners we read about, you pause, re-focus and intensify your efforts because going home is not an option. With this attitude, you would always choose to tackle your problems rather than give in or throw in the towel.

DAY 9 - ATTITUDE IS EVERYTHING

Exercise #1 Adjust Your Attitude

Read this and think about it before you do it. The exercise is to list 10 feelings or emotions you felt this week. A few examples are anger, anxiety, happiness, excitement and happiness. Rank them from 1 to 10, with 1 being the weakest, hurtful or the most unproductive and 10 being the strongest or the most productive.

I started this chart to demonstrate and help you re-frame those negative feelings to better serve your purpose and goals. If you are taking control of your life, then learning how to re-think your attitude is a SMART skill to learn. Consider these situations.

Strength 1 low to 10 strong	Emotion I felt this week	Trigger that started it	Something I can do to change it around to a better situation - or add to it and make it even stronger.
4	Sad	Grandma is sick	Make her a card, call her, send her a funny pic = change it to an 8 feeling, much better.
2	Angry	Bad grade on math test	Study next time, talk to teacher, get tutor = take control for a 7-8 feeling.
7-8	Strong Confident	Running	Keep it up, get new shoes when I can run 1 mile at a decent time = using motivation for booster.
	Healthy		Schedule time with friends to run = a 10 feeling guaranteed!

In this example, the person can turn those feelings around, or their attitude about them, if they take action in their lives. Reaching out to Grandma can turn sadness (4) around to happiness (8) very easily. The math situation is more complicated, but you have to be real and take responsibility for what you did not do. More importantly, what are you going to do to move it from that anger (2) to something decent (like a 7) or real success (like a 9 or 10)?

As for the good stuff, I always suggest kicking it up and notch or two. Build on those good feelings and strengthen bonds whenever you can. It adds more fun when friends or family join in your big adventure called life.

- **Make a list of 10 emotions you felt this past week, good and bad.**

- **Turn the list into the type of chart shown above.**

- **Start to look for patterns in your life. Adjust things to make life better.**

SCORECARD

1 Point for Each	Diet - Fitness - Water - Sleep - Attendance - Gratitude	
2 Points for Each	Attitude - Schoolwork - Warm-up Questions	Add It Up!
5 Points for Each	Daily Exercises	
10 Points	SMART Wakeup	DEPOSIT TOTAL FOR TODAY
BONUS Points	SMART Tasks	MY POINTS =

Coaching Tip From Ms. Peck –

Have you heard about the Turnaround Champion? They can take a hit from a poor performance and get a tune-up to turn it around next time. Don't let the past get in your way today, or tomorrow. You are building up resilience working these exercises. Pay attention to what you are doing, every day is brain training. Begin with your SMART Wakeup first thing in the morning. If you miss those points, it is ok, just use that slip up to tighten it up and turn it around tomorrow!

Day 10 - Opinions Are Not Facts

Warm-up Questions:

1. What are the differences between facts and opinions?
2. What are credible sources of information?
3. What makes a source of information reliable?
4. Why is it important to base your WebQuest on facts?
5. What are examples of places where you can get facts?

Power Words: Fact, Opinion

Fact: A piece of information that can be proven true or accurate.

Opinion: A person's statement of belief, judgment, or way of thinking about something.

Lesson:

When you want to set up an inquiry to talk about issues that affect a lot of people, it's great to learn how to get good information. Not every bit of information out there is credible. There is some info out there that is unreliable and inaccurate. This is because there are facts and opinions and you need to understand the differences and distinctions.

Facts are statements that can be proven as true.

Opinions exist because everyone always has something to say about everything. These days, because of the internet and social media, anyone can say what they like, and tons of people will read it and agree. If someone has a lot of followers they can say anything and people believe them, but that does not make their statement authentic or accurate. An opinion is still an opinion – just because many people are reading it does not make it a fact.

You can be sure that there's always a bias (or preference for one side) when someone is writing their opinions. That is because opinions are usually based on what we think or what we feel strongly about. Also, opinions can change. Sometimes, they change with our moods. For instance, we can say one thing when we're upset and then say something else when we are calmed down. For some people, they also change when their beliefs are no longer popular.

But facts are just the way they are. They don't change. We (authors/researchers/journalists) just uncover them or find out about them. Facts are usually things that have been tested or researched and proven over time. Information from sites that publish facts are considered reliable sources of information.

To get facts, you should turn to credible sources of information like longstanding news publications, academic texts, professional journals or articles written by experts in the field.

Making your WebQuest inquiries based only on opinions is dangerous. You wouldn't get a clear picture of what's going on. Your discussions wouldn't be as meaningful as you want them to and you wouldn't be able to draw logical conclusions.

Be sure to check out both sides of an issue. It might seem crazy to you, but the other side has reasons why they have their opinion. You have to be able to examine and evaluate multiple sides of problems, our project is a chance for you to test your smarts on your real life interests.

Exercise #1 - Gathering High Quality Information

Using a graphic organizer will help your brain gather and organize information from multiple sources. By now, you should be gathering information about 3 people facing the situation or social issue. When you are doing this research project, I want you to find both factual info and opinions from people directly involved.

Start your research today by seeking answers to the 5Ws of the situation. The 5Ws are often used by journalists to explain something in an easy way. The organizer has your questions in rows and uses a column for each of your teens and then you just fill in the info.

- **Who is involved? Who is against your point of view?**

- **When did it begin to be a problem? When did they get involved?**

- **Where – Did it start somewhere and then spread?**

- **What is the issue? What are the obstacles to get past?**

- **Why is it important to fix the problem? (opinion)**

DAY 10 - OPINIONS ARE NOT FACTS

As you take notes, you will want to capture some quotes from the people you are researching. If you can use the person's own words as part of your project, you will be using a credible source and score points. It is probably time to get more paper, this handbook is a guide for you to use while you research.

In this example, the student is worried about the environment and is going to fill in the background information they already know. As they gather more information, they will continue filling this grid in. The details will be separated between facts and opinions, and sources are being tracked for authority in the project.

Get the facts: WHO * WHEN * WHERE * WHAT

Get the opinions: WHY (need quotes)

At this point, the student started the WebQuest looking for other environmental activists or climate issues happening. The first activist making headlines is Greta Thunberg working on behalf of Climate Change. Here is some basic info, now it is time to go search online for other young people working on behalf of the environment (or whichever cause or issue you want).

As you know, thinking involves asking a lot of questions and digging for answers. In this example, the student lives in Florida and is concerned about the climate change effects of rising tides. They researched and learned about the flooding waters in Bangladesh and sinking city of Jakarta, Indonesia. Each location has different economic problems and government responses very different from Florida's. Lots of notes are being kept including the url addresses of news stories.

Who	**Greta Thunberg** **Against Oil Companies and Polluters**
When	**She started in 2018**
Where	**Sweden, Social Media, Website is Fridaysforfuture.org**
What	**Climate Crisis** **Started school strikes on Friday** **Time Magazine Person of the Year 2019**

Why	Raise awareness of the issue, promote ecological sustainability.
+	**"I don't want you to be hopeful. I want you to panic and act as if**
quote	**the house was on fire". "How dare you".**

This is a social issue workday and I want you to look back at the geography exercise we did on Day #8 and search in some of those countries. Also, look at the inquiry questions from Day #7 and update those as you dig deeper into the situation. The Social Studies standards want you to recognize any geographic features like mountains and rivers and DETERMINE IF they add to the social issue problem. How does the environment impact society?

I also want you to look at the maps of the countries you research. How many places have a road system as developed as ours? Some maps will show political, cultural or economic distinctions across the land. Keep exploring being safe online and keep track of every URL or domain address. The work you do today will pay off on Day #29, I guarantee!

Today's Scorecard

1 Point for Each	Diet - Fitness - Water - Sleep - Attendance - Gratitude	
2 Points for Each	Attitude - Schoolwork - Warm-up Questions	Add It Up!
5 Points for Each	Daily Exercises	
10 Points	SMART Wakeup	
BONUS Points	SMART Tasks	

DEPOSIT TOTAL FOR TODAY

MY POINTS =

Organizer Bonus +10 points for Research Notes on each of 3 people

Coaching Tip From Ms. Peck – *The 5Ws will help you focus and complete research this month. When you line up 3 different people's lives, an organizer can help you see patterns. Or number your research questions and answer them for all 3 people. There are similarities when you start to look for them. Gather first person comments or quotes from people who are making a difference, those will be powerful in your video.*

Day 11 - Ask Questions To Make Solutions

Warm-up Questions:

1. What social issue most affects you?

2. How do you dig deep into your problems?

3. What's the real cause of your hurdles or obstacles you face?

4. Who holds the other side from your point of view?

5. What will it take to resolve the problem?

Power Words: Personal Problem, Seven Layers Of Why

Personal Problem: The problems that originate within a person or their individual situation. These include a wide variety of financial, legal, alcohol or drug abuse, mental health, medical or family issues.

The Seven Layers Of Why: A technique used to peel away the multiple ways someone has handled a problem. The idea is to dig into the root causes, motivators or actions for an issue and seek alternatives to improve future growth.

Lesson:

Everyone has problems, and we have seen that our attitude to these problems determines if we are going to fix them or not. As a teen that wants to make your life better, you know choosing to find solutions is a better attitude to have. The first step is to adjust your thinking that it is possible to find a solution. It is not impossible, just hidden.

Now, there are many sides to every problem. Problems don't exist without reasons. This means that there is always a "why" to your problems. There's always something that the other side wants or needs, it could be simple like an apology or often something very complicated.

Problem solving is a skill that allows you to dig deep and find the root of problems.

Plenty of people try to live with their problems but often, they grow bigger and stop us from reaching our full potential. Time goes on and bad feelings turn into layers that can suffocate any hopes and dreams. Struggling people hold on to those layers and eventually, those hurt feelings become a shell around them.

Today, you are learning new ways of how to change the situation and make things better. Being in this CHALLENGE is helping you learn how to stop and think your way out of troubles or problems. If you are honest with yourself and practice this technique, I know you will see the benefits.

To get to these root causes and understand why things are happening the way they are, you'll have to peel off more and more layers of reasons. You need to ask a lot of questions so that you can tackle the real stuff underneath. Although it's sometimes emotional, asking these questions is worth it because they can be a way to finding lasting solutions.

When you are determined to solve a problem, you need to look for solutions in new ways. By using this technique, you are digging deep to find out why things happened the way they did.

The "7 Layers of Why" is when you ask the question over and over, but why this way, or why that way?

With each answer to the why question, you ask another why until the causes or roots of the problem are discovered. Ask the question over and over till you've peeled back the seven layers of "why". Each layer seeks to peel off the things that have masked the real cause of the pain you (or whomever) feel.

Let's illustrate this with an example. Freda Hill, 16 years old, has a problem concentrating in school. Here's how to use the 7 whys. The problem: She can't concentrate in class.

- Why (1): She sleeps off during classes.
- Why (2): She doesn't get enough sleep at night.
- Why (3): She's up late at night texting in a group chat.
- Why (4): She wants people to see her as cool.
- Why (5): She wants people to like and accept her.
- Why (6): She is lonely.
- Why (7): She's an only child. Her dad left and her mum is too busy to notice her. So, she craves acceptance and tries to fill that void by surrounding herself with lots of people all the time.

DAY 11 - ASK QUESTIONS TO MAKE SOLUTIONS

By using this technique, we can get a deeper insight into Freda's real problems. She is not concentrating in class, but that's a hint to a deeper issue – she's craving acceptance. If she didn't feel that way, she wouldn't have been texting at 2am about absolutely nothing. She would have been asleep by 11pm so that the next day, she would be awake and able to work at school.

If you flip this story and think about it in reverse, it is called the cause and effect relationships. Starting at the beginning and moving to today, what was the original problem? Her parents split up, what did Freda do? And then what happened, and what did Freda do? What can Freda do differently? (If it helps you to think about it flipped this way, use it.)

Now that we know what the real problem is, it is easier for Freda to find a solution to her problems. She may need therapy and a coach to help her embrace self-acceptance, teach her to focus and to make friends the right way. She can also learn how to talk with her mother about how she's feeling. If we didn't use the seven whys, we would never have uncovered the deeper issue that was really bugging her. Ok, now it is your turn.

Exercise #1 - What Is Really Driving The Problem?

Based on what you have learned, think about your social issue and peel off the layers using the seven whys until you get to the real problem society is facing. Let's practice this skill with the big problem that lots of people are facing, it will eliminate your stress of digging into your personal life this first time we try it.

Start writing out your social issue and peel back those layers about why this is important to you. This is a free writing activity, so just let it flow and keep asking why this keeps happening for so many people.

- The social issue of _____ is important to me because

- And then _____ is involved and they want _____
- And then _____ happened which is why they _____
- And then
- And then
- And then
- And so,

STUDENT SAMPLE TARGET: 1. Social issue of climate change and rising oceans impacts me living in Florida. 2. My community wants to develop the shoreline and I am worried about keeping the sea-grass and natural beaches secure. 3. In Bangladesh they can not build up against the rising water. 4. In Indonesia they are building concrete walls and in Bahamas they are planting more grasses and seabeds as natural walls. 5. Is it money for hotels or money for shoreline? 6. Government makes the laws 7. Non-profits try to help on the local level 8. How will the people decide which way to go?

Exercise #2 - Problem Solving Thinking Process

Problem solving is a process that makes you analyze your problems and helps you find solutions. In this exercise, you're going to be taking your free writing a step further. Here is a way you to help organize your thinking into an effective summary paragraph:

1. Identify the root causes and what is at stake if no solution is found.
2. State the problem clearly.
3. Why is it a problem? What kind of a solution will it need?
4. Who are the important people involved? What are they doing?
5. What obstacles need to be overcome in order to move forward?

Use this space to make a quick outline. Write down 1,2,3,4,5 quickly down the left margin, then add a few key words, or big ideas for each sentence. This quick step is about getting it all organized in your brain so you can start working it around in there. Think of the step as a round up, ok what do you know, big picture...

DAY 11 - ASK QUESTIONS TO MAKE SOLUTIONS

Ok, now you can really get your ideas into a tangible form. Get out and put on your SMART thinking hat. You are going to write a summary paragraph about your social issue using your research information. Just follow your outline!

- **Write a sentence addressing each of these topics. Be sure to give details and transitions between ideas.**

- **Review them and include a quote from one of your teen sources.**

- **Check for spelling and punctuation before you submit it for scoring today.**

Here is some space to get you started. Do not worry about your handwriting skills, they just need some practice being used. If you are typing, always check the recommendations before you turn it in now. Memorize those corrections because they will not be available when you are in a testing environment, grammar will be on you to know.

Today's Scorecard

1 Point for Each	Diet - Fitness - Water - Sleep - Attendance - Gratitude	
2 Points for Each	Attitude - Schoolwork - Warm-up Questions	Add It Up!
5 Points for Each	Daily Exercises	
10 Points	SMART Wakeup	
BONUS Points	SMART Tasks	

DEPOSIT TOTAL FOR TODAY

MY POINTS =

Coaching Tip From Ms. Peck - *Today is important to get your ideas flowing onto paper. At this point, neatness is not that important, thinking and putting all those ideas into print is the goal.*

When you practice the 7 Layers of Why, you can also try changing the question to – What if? You know, what if we tried _____, or what if this _____ was changed. This is a good way to propose changes or options while you are seeking a solution. Try to build on your ideas and include more details now, it will help your Catalyst For Change video later this month!

Day 12 - Must Have Study Skills

Warm-up Questions:

1. Describe your day planner, is it current?
2. Explain how you take notes while studying?
3. Can you write down what someone says while they are speaking?
4. Have you started using your study area setup on Day #6?
5. Which of your classes is the most difficult to understand? Why?

Power Words: Outline, Summary

Outline: A list of only the most important parts of (an essay, speech, plan, etc.).

Summary: A brief statement that gives the most important information about something.

Lesson:

Studying is more than just reading through your textbook. When you read through your schoolwork like you're reading through another comic book, chances are that you're not going to remember what you've read. Even if you do remember, it may just be bits and pieces here and there. That's not going to do you any good, is it?

There's a right way to study. There's also a wrong way to study.

Studying without taking notes isn't studying at all. When you study, you have a goal. You want to understand what you were taught in class. You also want to be able to apply it when you need to. That shows you have learned the concept or the subject that was talked about.

Experts say we remember what we write down a lot more than what we just read. Building memory strength, or intelligence can be done by capturing your thinking in any way possible. It can be expressed using words, graphs or flowcharts; the point is to process information, draw conclusions or put 2+2 together. Everyone who wants to succeed at school has to take their notes during class, and then study very seriously.

Note taking is putting the information down onto paper (or digitally), in your own words. It is important to get good notes during class lectures and every learning opportunity you have. Like I said earlier, it helps you remember. It also gives you a chance to think and process the information and write what you've learned in your own words.

When you are studying, you should be sitting at a desk – we talked about creating a unique study space and have an additional notebook/materials by your side. I want you to remember to take this study time seriously and NEVER rush the work you need to accomplish.

To do a good job on the Catalyst Project, you'll follow the information trail and summarize what you have been able to learn or understand as you go. Write down the main ideas and key details like names and the domain addresses where you found the information on the WebQuest. It is best to practice critical thinking and summarize the material in your own words. Identify possible quotations from credible sources because it helps you keep track of who is who.

These four tips will make studying easier and your grades improve!

1. Learning Goal - Before studying, it's important to ask yourself what you hope to learn or understand after the session. This is going to become your target or goal. It would help you pay close attention to what you are studying because you will seek to answer the questions and understand the concepts without wasting any time.

2. Break it Down - As you read through your schoolwork and take down notes, pay close attention to how facts are presented. You have to separate the opinions and gather quotations from qualified sources. Read a paragraph or two and stop to make a note.

Notes should follow a type of pattern based on how the information was presented. Look for the organization or text structure of what you read and follow it as your guide. You can use the Table of Contents to help you see the framework or author's outline. Some texts include paragraph numbering to help you find your place or subtitles to show groupings.

DAY 12 - MUST HAVE STUDY SKILLS

Yesterday you made an outline for writing. Today think about it in reverse for reading. Here is a typical example to help you see and better understand the outline format.

1. Introductions are the overview and statement of situation,
2. The main material will be in the body section.
    1. It is the longest and
    2. broken into logical sections
3. The ending section wraps it up, often makes a call to action.

3. Use graphic organizers. When you put similar concepts together on a grid, it helps you make those visual learning connections. Think about how one piece of info leads to another piece of info until you make sense of the whole picture. Use a flowchart as you study. I will use a highlighter to draw how concepts fit together, or color code key ideas.

4. Summarize in your own words. Write down your thinking about why or how you reached your summary. Describe or explain what you just read. If it's a mathematical equation that you are working, write down the step by step directions to solve the problem.

When you do a great job taking your notes and gathering all the information, it makes them perfect for studying for tests and exams. That's because you will capture all the crucial points the teachers make and when you write them in your words, it helps you understand better and remember later.

Exercise #1 - Practice The Lesson

Write an outline for the lesson text you just read. Add the details in your own words following the example above.

Exercise #2 Catalyst Project Summary Paragraphs

- Spend some time working on your Catalyst Project today. Update your notes and graphic organizers to improve the amount and quality of your research.

- Write a summary paragraph for each of the teenagers you found and have been learning about. Explain who they are and how they are working to improve the social problem in their community. One teen paragraph scores the daily points.

- Catalyst Bonus: Each summary earns you the 10 points today, so writing all three is 20 more bonus points for you!!

- Hint: look back at that paragraph summary example and rubric from Day #8 and Day #11.

Today's Scorecard

1 Point for Each	Diet - Fitness - Water - Sleep - Attendance - Gratitude	
2 Points for Each	Attitude - Schoolwork - Warm-up Questions	Add It Up!
5 Points for Each	Daily Exercises	
10 Points	SMART Wakeup	
BONUS Points	SMART Tasks	

DEPOSIT TOTAL FOR TODAY

MY POINTS =

Catalyst Bonus +20 for two more summary paragraphs

Coaching Tip From Ms. Peck –

Hey – Heads Up! SMART Task tomorrow so, be sure you are ready to go with your Smart Start Wakeup. It might be time to update that message or re-focus yourself on success. Make any changes necessary to improve your performance. Sometimes, a smart start begins the night before!

Day 13 - My Words Matter

Warm-up Questions:

1. How well do you speak? What kind of words do you use?
2. What does your social media profile say about you?
3. Are you sending out the right kind of non-verbal messages?
4. How do people feel after listening or talking to you?
5. What is your best character trait? Explain

Power Words: Communication, Positive

Communication: The act or process of using words, sounds, signs, body language or behaviors to express your ideas, thoughts, feelings and so on.

Positive: Something useful or something that has a good effect.

Lesson:

How you speak says a lot about who you are on the inside. The words we use and the way we say them show people the kind of person we are. Ugly, hurtful words are spoken by ugly people. This is because you can't give what you don't have.

If you are full of meanness, you would show it in the things you say. If you find that you are always saying words that tear other people down, chances are that you're a mean person, and that's not cool. You would always make people feel terrible around you. Ask yourself, "If people talked to me the way I talked to them, would I be happy"?

Words can build you up and words can destroy you.

Be kind to yourself and to others. Think good thoughts about yourself and about others because your words begin as thoughts. Then, as you open your mouth to speak, let your words uplift people and make them feel better about themselves. Remember your personal bank account and always try to make deposits.

Never say things that would hurt people or make them question their worth. Never say things that would tear people down or make them cower and hide. Be positive. Spread love and light. Spread happiness and joy.

Learn to use the magic words – please, thank you and sorry. Use them often and appropriately. Also learn to talk like a winner. Practice a phrase so it is easy and natural to say. It doesn't cost anything to be nice, but it does a world of good when you're polite. This goes for what you say to yourself too.

Be clear in your communication. Don't say things you don't mean and assume people would not care or think you were joking. As much as possible, don't give people a chance to misquote or misunderstand you. If you make a mistake, admit it immediately and apologize.

Let your body language always match your speech. When you are happy, communicate it clearly. When you want to show someone that they're welcome, let them see it. Smile genuinely when you say hello. Give thumbs up when you encourage someone. Wave when you want to say goodbye and mean every compliment you pay.

Sometimes, people smile at you and you don't feel like smiling back because their smile is like the Joker's. There's a lot of hidden stuff underneath. Don't be like that. Let your smile spring from your heart. Give it freely and genuinely.

There is a lot of negativity out there. Choose not to be a part of it. Use your social media to spread joy and laughter. Don't be a troll or a bully. Rather, use your space and influence to connect with smart people, share ideas and spread positive vibes.

Exercise #1 - Only Use The Good Ones

Today you are going to upgrade your vocabulary in your head. First, make a list of 5 things you say to yourself regularly. Do you have a name you call yourself when something goes wrong? What negative things come to mind when you think back about the past few days? Jot it down here.

DAY 13 - MY WORDS MATTER

Next, you are going to turn around those stinking words into something sweet. This is also about your new mindset and taking control of your thoughts. Remember we learned about re-framing your thoughts. This is re-framing your vocabulary. Here are a few words as examples, but I want you to really be honest and creative.

This work is about creating your future, so do take it seriously. Self-sabotage can be stopped when you stop and think about it. You could even write down sentences like - I used to say _____ but now I think _____ is a better way of looking at it. Consider adding some of these new uplifting vocabulary words into your SMART Wakeup.

Old Negative Stinking Thinking	New Sweeter Kinder Mindset	My Old Stinking Thinking	My Smarter Mindset
Lost	Searching		
Failed	Learning something		
Angry	Motivated to change		
Lazy	Unfocused		
Loser	Leader - go find something new!		

Exercise #2 - Upgrade My Social Media - SMART Task

The image you project on social media is a reflection of who you really are as a person. Examine your stream of postings on your social media. Does it reflect the amazing person you are? Do your pictures and comments highlight your life and awesome future? Now is the time to improve what you communicate to the world. Your words create your future, so always use the best ones.

- Delete the garbage from the low road of life and focus on the higher road and better future.
- Cancel your negative feed and go find some positive inspiration to boost you every day.
- Change your habit of posting ugly memes or jokes to posting stories of success or dreams of places around the world. Repeat after me – "My words matter and only my best will do!"

Show the world how amazing you are. All eyes are on you, so smile with confidence. When your profile is ready for Ms. Peck to see, make a post on the websites SmartStartChallenge.com and AskMsPeck.com to earn double the SMART Task points.

Today's Scorecard

1 Point for Each	Diet - Fitness - Water - Sleep - Attendance - Gratitude	
2 Points for Each	Attitude - Schoolwork - Warm-up Questions	Add It Up!
5 Points for Each	Daily Exercises	
10 Points	SMART Wakeup	*DEPOSIT TOTAL FOR TODAY*
BONUS Points	SMART Tasks	*MY POINTS =*

SMART TASK +25 Bonus for Social Media Upgrade

Coaching Tip From Ms. Peck –

Speaking of the things you put into yourself, what did you eat for breakfast today? How many hours did you sleep last night? Self-care is important and something we need to make a priority. Give your body respect and take good care of it every day. Recognizing and giving thanks encourages more good to you. Pay attention!! You are creating your best future right now!!

Day 14 - Dump That Toxic Mess

Warm-up Questions:

1. How do you react to gossip?
2. Have you ever been bullied in school?
3. Do you have a go-to phrase for bullies?
4. How do you react if you witness someone being bullied?
5. Have you ever been in a heated argument?

Power Words: Gossip, Bullies

Gossip: A person who often talks about the private details of other people's lives. It also means a rumor or report of an intimate nature.

Bully: Someone who is mean to others who are not as tough as they are.

Lesson:

While you're trying hard to become a better person, there will always be people who just don't want you living your best life; they are always trying to know what you're up to and trying to put you down. They are usually up to no good. They get their greatest joy when others are afraid of them. I'm talking about your school bullies and the gossips.

I'm sure you're tired of their antics and you've been wondering why they won't leave you or the other teens alone. Well, here's their little secret: Many times, they don't feel too good about themselves and so they try to project their insecurities on others. They walk around acting like they're better than everyone else but deep down, how they really feel about themselves is the exact opposite. Haters are just full of hate.

If this applies to you, it must stop immediately.

Stick to the high road, always.

First, you must never take their insults personally. You must never let them drag you down to their level. Do not argue with them. Never reply to them with profanity or use bad words. Whenever they want to have a row with you, try your best to IGNORE THEM.

If you find a way to ignore them or show them that they're not all that, they'll quit messing with you. When you do not give them a reaction, they will stop trying. Think about those celebrities who just smile and wave – you do the same thing. If the bully ends up feeling foolish anytime they cross paths with you, with time, they'll leave you alone.

It's the same with people who gossip. Many times, they're shallow and do not feel happy about themselves. They feel better when they tell negative stories about people. When there's gossip about you, just ignore it. That's always the best thing to do. Don't deny or affirm the story. Act like you don't care because you actually shouldn't. Why should you bother about people who are so focused on others that they can't get a grip on their own lives?

One thing that gives bullies and gossips power over people is the feeling of fear they create in you. When they know how much they get to you and how afraid you are of them, they'll keep trying to get under your skin. That stops when you stop letting their words get to you.

The best way to do that is to stop internalizing what they say. Stop believing their words. Rather, understand that what they're saying is a reflection of how they see themselves. Just like the good words yesterday, what they say is who they are.

Many times, they are jealous of who you are and how much you are taking responsibility for your future. Deep down, I bet some of them wish they were you. People get jealous and that is on them, do not let them bring you down.

To handle them perfectly, stick to your position and hold your head up high. Exhale and think for a second and try to feel sorry for their miserable lives. Then, be confident and assert yourself and say in a big voice "just stop wasting time."

When they stop in their tracks, you freeze them with something like – "thank you for recognizing my ability to do _____ but just stop wasting time." Look them in the eye and make your statement loud and clear. When you do this consistently, the bullies and gossips will give up. They would either get on your side or just stop messing with you.

DAY 14 - DUMP THAT TOXIC MESS

Exercise #1 - Prepare For Battle

First, always stick to the high road and out of the gutter where they are. Today, I want you to develop a go-to phrase for any gossip and bullies you have to deal with. Think about who usually has some kind of put down or hassle and create a SMART response. Practice it and get better prepared for a battle of wits.

Write your own response here:

*Name _____

Exercise #2 - Dump The Toxic

You control what goes into your beautiful brain and today is the day to get rid of all the garbage. You know those ugly spirited people or hateful influencers that have become popular lately - they have got to GO!

This is another social media upgrade - go delete those people who do not encourage or motivate you to greatness. Dump the people who tell lies to make them look good, or hide the truth to protect themselves. This is easy for those "friends" you have never really met in person, delete them.

Trust me, I only follow positive and inspirational people in my social media feed. And, my private life is private from my life on social media. This is about developing our moral compass or an inner foundation of strength. I have made the commitment to making deposits in my internal bank every chance I get and I hope you do too.

Make the list of people who need to be let go or unsubscribed. Go do it.

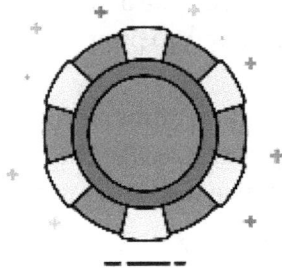

Today' Scorecard

1 Point for Each	Diet - Fitness - Water - Sleep - Attendance - Gratitude	
2 Points for Each	Attitude - Schoolwork - Warm-up Questions	**Add It Up!**
5 Points for Each	Daily Exercises	
10 Points	SMART Wakeup	
BONUS Points	SMART Tasks	

DEPOSIT TOTAL FOR TODAY

MY POINTS =

Coaching Tip From Ms. Peck –

Another toxic person to dump is the cheat. Someone who copies or takes other people's work or any shortcut or fraud they can find – they have got to go! Do not let them bring you down to their level thinking it is ok. Cheaters only win in the short run. Life is a marathon, develop good character to go the distance.

And, guess what?? Tomorrow you make it through two rounds of exercises that are helping you get a smarter start on your future. I bet you are really feeling those brain muscles getting stronger every day!

Day 15 - Developing My Point Of View

Warm-up Questions:

1. Have you located 3 people and researched their experiences with the issue?
2. How is your research helping you understand the situation here?
3. What did you find as a possible solution for your community?
4. Can you explain your values about what is important in life?
5. What have you learned about yourself in the past week?

Power Words: Values, Choices

Values: A quality (of human behavior) we take very seriously.

Choices: Things we decide to do.

Lesson:

Values are things we take seriously or things we see as important. Values are abstract things – things we cannot see or touch, but they affect the way we think, the decisions we make and the reasons we do things. They are what makes us all different as we don't have them in the same kinds of ways. Without values, our lives lose meaning and we will just do things because everyone else does.

The right kind of values inspire you to make good choices. They make you head in the right direction for your life. They inspire you to be productive and to make decisions that would affect your future in a positive way. They also inspire you to make healthy decisions, think better of yourself and work on your goals.

Knowing your values helps establish your point of view about life.

There are some kinds of values that steer you in the wrong direction. The bad ones can inspire you to be lazy and to focus on things that don't count. They take you far away from your goals, make you do things you shouldn't do and get you into a lot of trouble. These are the kinds of values to stay away from.

Many times, we get caught up in wrong habits or wrong decisions because we haven't decided what our values are or figured out what we want them to be. If we do not know our point of view, we have a hard time making good decisions. The longer we stay in those moments, the more bad decisions we make.

When you decide to choose your values and stick to them, you will start thinking before making bad decisions.

When you recognize or identify your values, you can easily create a path to lead you to your dream life. This path would guide the things you do, the places you go and the kind of people you hang out with. If you have a positive perspective that things can work out, then they will, because your values and goals are aligned.

If you want to graduate as an honor student and head off to college, your core values would have to be discipline and focus. These values would play out in your attitude towards schoolwork. Because of your focus, you wouldn't skip classes. As a disciplined person, you would be at school on time. You would also take your schoolwork pretty seriously – you'll study for your midterms and for your exams. You would work on your school projects and turn them in before deadlines.

Your values also affect your life outside of school. Your attitude to other people, the kind of things you choose to do or enjoy, tell a lot about who you are and the kind of things you value or take seriously. If you volunteer at homeless shelters, babysit or walk your neighbor's dogs, it shows you're someone who values helping people.

If, on the other hand, you stay home all-day obsessing about celebrities and wishing you had a better life, you're probably someone who needs to re-think how you handle your life. This is the SMART START CHALLENGE remember, so get smarter about what you value and where you put your focus and energy.

If you have had the wrong kind of values before now, you can fix it and need to immediately. There is a story of a ship's captain crossing the ocean and he was less than 1 degree off on the compass and missed the target destination by over 1,000 miles. When you are young, your life is like that ship on the ocean. Tighten up your compass.

DAY 15 - DEVELOPING MY POINT OF VIEW

Decide to value qualities that make you a better person. The qualities or character traits that inspire you to be fair, to work hard at your goals, to be kind, to give, to care about people and to be considerate. These qualities require a lot of discipline to nurture, but their results are worthwhile and lasting.

Exercise #1 - Update My Point Of View About School

This past week, you have learned about habits, attitudes, problem solving and so on. I know these lessons are beginning to change the way you see things. Now, think about your school problem, or whatever has been holding you down. How is it changing? Have you figured out a way to tackle it? What kind of things could be done differently to help turn it around? I know you have been thinking...

Write out your thoughts – how do you want school, or your education to be? Where do you want to be in the future?
What are you willing to change?

- *My values about school and what I want in life includes:*_____

- *My long-term education is going to include things like:* _____

- *My learning goals for this year include:* _____

Exercise #2 - Catalyst for Change Project Update

Review your notes about the project and add your critical thinking today. Think about how each person is working to improve their local situation. Ask yourself the 7 questions about why they face the same problem and what can be done to help. How is it different living outside the USA? How are the situations similar? Do they have ideas you could implement here?

- **Make a list of reasons or ideas we share.**
- **Explain what needs to change to work toward a solution.**
- **Write out your ideas in sentences to get them onto paper.**
- **Working your hand and your brain together makes it stronger.**

Today's Scorecard

1 Point for Each	Diet - Fitness - Water - Sleep - Attendance - Gratitude	
2 Points for Each	Attitude - Schoolwork - Warm-up Questions	**Add It Up!**
5 Points for Each	Daily Exercises	
10 Points	SMART Wakeup	*DEPOSIT TOTAL FOR TODAY*
BONUS Points	SMART Tasks	*MY POINTS =*

Bonus completion of Round #1 and Round #2 = 14 days of work + 50 points

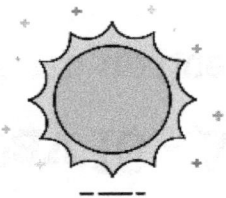

Coaching Tip From Ms. Peck –

Be sure that you always use the uplifting words when you speak with yourself in your head. Take a minute and look for little things in your day that bring you joy and give a little thanks. It can almost be a game if you start encouraging or showing appreciation to random people. For example, if the cashier has a cute necklace or your mail carrier delivers a giant package – say something nice and watch them smile. Give it a try. Happiness can be contagious.

Day 16 - Making A Statement

Warm-up Questions:

1. What do you think about yourself?
2. What do people say about you?
3. What was the last thing you posted on social media?
4. How do you relate with new people you meet?
5. What's your story? Describe yourself.

Power Words: Your Story, Vibes

Your Story: The things (experiences, habits, values) you tell yourself and other people.

Vibes: How your presence makes people feel.

Lesson:

As people, we are constantly giving off vibes, consciously or unconsciously – some good, some not so great. These vibes are what make people decide who they think we are. If you are a person who constantly shuts everyone out, stutters when people ask you questions and never wants to do anything, people would think you're afraid, shy or you just don't have anything nice to say.

If, on the other hand, you are outspoken, confident and cheerful, and you're always putting your best foot forward, people would think you're smart and talented. They might even think you have great leadership qualities and entrust you with responsibilities, even if you don't think you do.

It is important to understand first impressions and the kind of vibes you give off.

Consciously or unconsciously, the things you project to the outside world become your story over time. The things you project by the moods you're constantly in, your words, your attitude, your body language, your clothes, your hairstyle and even the posts you make on social media, will shape people's opinion about you.

Being intentional or choosing what kind of vibes you send out helps you tell your story to the world – in your own words and in your own way. Letting yourself give all sorts of confusing or conflicting vibes by just doing things on a whim, makes your story subject to whoever is watching you display those moods and actions. That is not cool. Be smart, take control of your life.

It's your life and you should be the one telling your own story. You should show people who you really believe you are. Control what you project, and you control your future. Don't be labelled by the silly, confused version of you that people have created because of a little slip or your misunderstanding of how important this is.

It is okay if you haven't been particular about this in the past. It's also okay if you have given off the wrong vibes before now. Part of growing up is making mistakes, learning from them and deciding to do better. You know who you are, let's go adjust that statement.

Don't let your fears or past experiences keep you from re-writing your story. You know who you were, who you are right now and who you want to be. You also know the steps you're taking right now to make sure you become the "you" you've always dreamed about. Let that be what you project – a person who is excited about who you are, and the growth process you are going through right now.

You are what you say you are, not what the bullies and the haters have said. You are the only person who gets to decide who or what you're going to be. That's because only you have the power to work towards making your dream a reality. Know this and be confident in it. Let those good thoughts you have about yourself show in your speech, in your body language and in the way you talk. So, hold your head high and project the "you" you want to be seen.

Exercise #1 - What's Your First Impression?

Complete the following sentences and consider what kind of impression you make on people. The idea is to improve your reputation by changing those negative things people perceive about you into positive ones. If these answers are not positive and uplifting, or getting a good reaction, they probably need to be adjusted.

DAY 16 - MAKING A STATEMENT

- Most people would say I have a _____ attitude because I act like _____.
- My physical style or look could be described as
  _____.
- When I meet new people, I tell them I am interested in
  _____.
- Do people know your greatest strength or superpower is _____? Why or why not?
- What part of your story needs to be updated to match the new SMARTER you?
  _____.

Exercise #2 - Rewrite Your Future – SMART Task

Yes, this is a metaphor because it refers to one thing while mentioning another. Just think for a minute. Reflect on who you have been this past year and who you are on your way to becoming. You have chosen to change your outlook and the things you project to the outside world. Fourteen days ago, you had a future, now your point of view has changed, and you are going to rewrite your future.

In this exercise, you are going to identify the negative things you have projected by your speech, actions or body language. You are also going to write down the vocabulary you have used in the past to describe yourself. Today, you are going to choose to change your story by writing down the things you're going to say and do differently.

Fill in the spaces with the info, and then write up your new story and post it where you can see it every morning. Consider adding it to your daily Smart Start Wakeup practice. I want you to put your best self out in front and make that statement, be bold and proud.

My Old Story: In the past, I saw myself as ...

I said and did things like ...

I projected myself as ...

TODAY - My New Story: I will say things like ...

I will do things like ...

I will project myself as ...

Exercise #3 - Make The Best Statement

You have already updated your social media feed with good content. Now, it is time to adjust your own profile. You know those pictures and posts that need to be deleted. I want you to promise yourself that you will change your ways. The world runs on the energy you put out there, so be sure it is the most powerful message and you will see success start to happen.

Once you have a fabulous profile, you should create a post and tag Ask Ms. Peck on your social media.
Tell your new story to the world and get bonus points today!

Today's Scorecard

1 Point for Each	Diet - Fitness - Water - Sleep - Attendance - Gratitude	
2 Points for Each	Attitude - Schoolwork - Warm-up Questions	**Add It Up!**
5 Points for Each	Daily Exercises	
10 Points	SMART Wakeup	DEPOSIT TOTAL FOR TODAY
BONUS Points	SMART Tasks	MY POINTS =

Bonus 25+ SMART Task for My New Story

Coaching Tip from Ms. Peck -

Awesome Job! Put your new story out there and be proud of the person you are becoming. You have a new perspective of the world and what you want out of it. I am serious, only look forward to that exact direction you want to reach. Never look back. Focus. Promise yourself to never tell that old story again, ever.

Day 17 - Seeking Common Ground

Warm-up Questions:

1. Who are the people involved in your Catalyst For Change Project?
2. What do they want to achieve when the solution to the problem is found?
3. What are the barriers to finding a solution?
4. What is the common ground or something everyone can agree upon?
5. How can you go look for, or seek out this common ground?

Power Words: Stakeholders, Common Ground

Stakeholders: Those people who may be affected by or have an effect on a problem.

Common Ground: In a conflict, the small things we can agree upon even if we disagree on the larger issue or proposal/solution.

Lesson:

Today, I want to focus on the big social issue you have chosen as your project. Let's talk about the big picture first so you will understand today's lesson and then hopefully, be able to use it.

When a social problem exists, there are lots of people it affects. These are the stakeholders. They are the people who are most impacted by a particular problem or social issue. These issues aren't just something they hear about in the news or read in books. It is their current reality. They are living it every day.

Seek to listen and learn with an open mind and heart.

Stakeholders can be people who influence or affect a problem positively or negatively. Sometimes people have something to gain when the problem gets worse and they would lose big time if the problem went away. It can be about money and sometimes the corporations (or politicians) hold the power.

Many times, problems last longer than they should because some people benefit from it. For the Catalyst Project, we have to research both sides of the issue. First we will focus on the stakeholders who the problem affects – like the teens you found in your online research.

Every stakeholder has something they want. Many times, when someone has a problem we naturally assume that they just want out. It isn't always true. Some people want pity. Some want money to solve their problems. Others want the problem to be a basis on which they get favors and goodwill from people. And yes, some people actually want to find solutions.

It's always good to know what people want – not what you think they want. You have to ask people about their problem and then really listen. That way, you can provide an effective solution they would enjoy and benefit from. Sometimes, people have multiple problems. The one that hits them the hardest is usually the one they tend to focus on.

For example, people travelling through the desert don't usually care about internet wi-fi at a rest area. Their priority is usually water. They wish they could get water because it is so dry and hot. If you give them a great high-speed internet connection, they probably would not appreciate it.

Whenever we want to solve problems, we encounter all sorts of barriers. This is because there are different things that try to stop us from achieving our goals. Sometimes, it's our environment or big things out of our control. It could also be old-fashioned government policies, or the way people are biased and treated differently from others.

So, the first step to helping stakeholders get what they want is to identify the barriers (things or people) that need to be resolved.

When you find those barriers, your first instinct should be to shatter them. While that's really smart and zealous thinking, it isn't always possible, at least not immediately. Considering another perspective or viewpoint is a skill we are practicing. There are two sides to every story, be sure to hear both. The thing to do is to find common ground so both parties can have a win-win situation.

DAY 17 - SEEKING COMMON GROUND

A common ground is something the stakeholders and the people upholding the barriers can agree upon. When you go over both sides of an argument, brainstorm, dig deep and find a footing or some point that favors both sides, you have found a common ground. A common ground isn't always an easy thing to find, but it usually solves the problem without causing any more problems.

An example would be negotiating with your parents for a reward when you complete this SMART START CHALLENGE. Think about things both of you want to accomplish - something easy like you are getting up on time for school. It's something they want you to do and it's something you are practicing here with your morning routine. Both of you win and because this is happening, that makes it easy for you to find a way to celebrate the better YOU.

Exercise #1 - The Big Picture

In your service project, who are the stakeholders and what do they want? What are the barriers preventing what they want? Where is the common ground?

This is critical thinking and it takes a lot of time to work through all the different questions and ideas. Social problems exist because they're often controversial and can be hard for the "other side" to understand. Finding something in common is the strategy today. Often a plea for the sake of "our children" or "our homes" or another personal subject is effective. You need something everyone wants. Start writing your ideas here, brainstorm to get many creative thoughts as you work to find a solution.

The Stakeholders ...

What they want ...

Barriers ...

Common ground ...

Exercise #2 - Breaking Down Your Challenge

A graphic organizer helps your brain see relationships differently and improves your critical thinking. Every time you chart out the issues, it becomes easier to find solutions. This will help you lay it out before your eyes. You can draw a vertical line down the middle and stack up your ideas next to your opposition. What is your perspective compared to theirs?

Think about your life and the stakeholders you have. Think about the people who are invested in you and your future. If there are problems with these relationships, it can be difficult to find a solution, but this strategy can help you.

Go and talk with the people involved. Seek to listen and learn from them and their experiences. Trust me, the problem will not go away on its own. You need to work together to resolve conflicts quickly.

Fill-in this chart and explore your stakeholders' wants, their viewpoints and the barriers you face. Be creative and honest with yourself about what you need to do in order to find a solution. Find the common ground and you can find a solution to whatever the problem may be. You may need to brainstorm options. This may take some time, thinking is a process your brain has to do.

Problem: Dig into it and find the real, root of the issue.	What is your position?	What is your opposition?
Who thinks this is a problem and why?		
What are the barriers to finding a solution?		
Why haven't previous solutions worked?		

DAY 17 - SEEKING COMMON GROUND

What do both of you want to accomplish?

What could be given up or changed to make the common ground happen?

Where is a win-win for both sides?

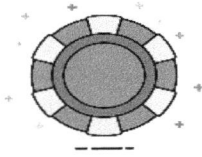

Today's Scorecard

1 Point for Each	Diet - Fitness - Water - Sleep - Attendance - Gratitude	
2 Points for Each	Attitude - Schoolwork - Warm-up Questions	**Add It Up!**
5 Points for Each	Daily Exercises	
10 Points	SMART Wakeup	*DEPOSIT TOTAL FOR TODAY*
BONUS Points	SMART Tasks	*MY POINTS =*

Equipment Room Alert – Filling in this graphic organizer is great for this exercise. Next time you need some clear thinking, look at the end of the handbook. Any tool that can help you think and find solutions is really smart to use!

Coaching Tip From Ms. Peck –

When you are looking for common ground or analyzing a problem, you need to be neutral or open with your thinking. You need to recognize another point of view and listen. I warn you to consider any stakeholders' perspective, but do not hold it against them. Give respect because it will be returned.

The change you want to see begins with you, so start by giving your opponents a chance; listen and learn from them. To really get a fresh chance at a new solution, it means having clean thinking without negative baggage or bias. Learn from the past but leave it there.

Day 18 - Training My Brain

Warm-up Questions:

1. Do you multi-task at school, or while doing schoolwork?
2. How much time do you spend online with entertainment, gaming or social media?
3. Have you ever tried meditation?
4. Have you ever sat still for thirty minutes?
5. How do you think meditation impacts the way you think?

Power Words: Critical Thinking, Meditation

Critical Thinking: Analyzing and evaluating issues objectively to form judgment.

Meditation: A quiet practice where a person uses a technique to train attention and awareness. It helps people achieve a mentally clear and emotionally calm and stable state.

Lesson:

Every day, we train our brains with the things we do and pay attention to. By training your brain, you are teaching your brain how to respond to situations. What you pay attention to decides or inspires how your brain will respond in hard times. If you spend all day watching series on "Netflix" or "Snapchatting", you are not helping your brain become any better.

When you are faced with problems, your brain will first respond with panic, anxiety and fear because of what you have been putting into your mind. But when you choose to pay attention to things that are important – like your schoolwork, books on problem solving and so on, you are teaching your brain to respond in a better, more logical way.

Critical thinking is a skill you need to practice. Very often, you need to use it when you are faced with difficult situations or problems. When you have some challenges and you decide to calm down to try and understand what it's about and find a solution, you are thinking. When you dig deep and try to get to the root cause, identify the barriers to finding a solution and so on, you are thinking critically.

When you think critically, you are not worrying or getting panicked. Instead, you're trying to find a solution to the problem. You dig deep and you also ask questions — using the seven whys. Then, you try to put bits and pieces of info together to be able to arrive at the bigger picture. At first, you may not be any good at this but with time, you will improve on your skills and find more ways to think better.

Stillness and meditation can help you gather and improve your mind.

Stillness and meditation are mindful practices or routines that calm your mind and help you think clearly. They are skills that can help you get through panic and fear. Instead of getting all worked up, you breathe in deeply and meditate or sit still.

Because they're not common things to do (although more people are learning about them now), a lot of people have a hard time practicing them. Both routines require lots of discipline and focus. They also need you to sit in a place for more than ten minutes. If you usually want to be messing with something, scrolling texts or talking on social media, I suggest you begin meditation today. These routines help you train your brain to become better every day.

Meditation and stillness are similar but there are some differences. People can meditate without being completely still. There are some forms of meditation that require you to say something (like OooMmmm) to keep your mind focused. Listening to guided meditation can lead you to a sort of happiness. Saying prayers can also be a type of meditation, repeating bible verses has comforted people for centuries.

But you can also be completely still during meditation. In stillness, you are calm, quiet and you let your body relax. Then, you ease into the process and let your mind wander into the deepest kinds of thoughts. Both practices help your brain stay sharp.

Although you can think critically without meditating, I think it works a lot better when you meditate first. Many people believe that meditation is spiritual and that the effects transcend our normal bodies. Centering or gathering yourself, for just a moment or 30+ minutes is a thinking booster that works!

Being able to control your mind when your thoughts are racing is a critical skill to develop.

DAY 18 - TRAINING MY BRAIN

Exercise #1 - Practice Meditation For Stillness

Anyone can meditate. All you need to do is to find a quiet place, strike a relaxed position, either lying down or in a comfortable chair, and quiet your mind. You want to turn off your mind and all the thoughts racing through it. When you learn how to calm your mind, you will gain incredible mental strength.

When you are relaxed, thoughts will come into your mind, acknowledge them and then let them go. Imagine each thought going out of you and calmness or peace coming in. Imagine you are in your favorite location and just enjoy the peace.

Set a timer for 5 minutes to try it then, describe the experience.

You should also consider adding time for meditation into your daily Smart Start Wakeup. You can find plenty of guided meditations that can help you with many personal problems. Sometimes, just calling out those negative thoughts can make them disappear.

When you have practiced meditation or stillness today, take a few minutes to write down your thoughts. I suggested 5 minutes, some people meditate for 30 minutes or longer. What did it feel like? Did you quiet your mind into a peaceful mental place? Describe what you were struggling to quiet. Try it again and explain what you experienced the second time.

Exercise #2 - My Mental Awareness Alert

The study of Analytic Psychology has proven that our brains work on a conscious (alert) and subconscious (without our knowledge) level. What you perceive or see involves more than just your eyes. On a conscious level, you may see a red rose, but the subconscious says it is love and passion. As you learn to quiet your mind, your subconscious may be sending you a lot of messages.

Carl Jung was a Swiss psychologist and one of the first to explore a phenomenon known as coincidences. He theorized that the thoughts people sometimes get, like a deja-vu, is your brain at work processing information. Memories and life events totally unrelated seem to align and can leave someone feeling in awe. It has been described as a synchronous feeling of energy. Others describe it like feeling a sign from God or the universe.

If you experience it, become still and take note of what you are experiencing. The brain is processing information which is a good thing. Thoughts about your home, school or relationships often overlap and can hold secrets about the mystery in your life. This is also true for dreams while you are sleeping. When you wake, observe how you mind is working.

Not all coincidences are a big revelation, most are a little nudge that you are on the right path. When I experience them, I feel confident that things are right with me. The more you notice the synchronicity happening, the more you will attract and experience these little miracles of brain power.

Think back to any of those strange experiences you have had, maybe when you lost something and then remember seeing it exactly. Or times when a friend mentions a new song and now the radio seems to play it all the time. If you notice it, stop and think about it because that is your brain working.

Scientists are researching brain functions and finding out amazing things about our mental health. Daydreaming is another sign of our subconscious mind taking a little control. Just be aware, these are thoughts that can be productive.

Describe any experiences you may have had and keep your mind alert to all kinds of ideas!

Today's Scorecard

1 Point for Each	Diet - Fitness - Water - Sleep - Attendance - Gratitude	
2 Points for Each	Attitude - Schoolwork - Warm-up Questions	**Add It Up!**
5 Points for Each	Daily Exercises	
10 Points	SMART Wakeup	DEPOSIT TOTAL FOR TODAY
BONUS Points	SMART Tasks	MY POINTS =

Coaching Tip From Ms. Peck -

Carl Jung had several theories about people and how their minds process information. Jung believed people create their personas, or identities based on their social position and what they wanted to achieve in life. The theory that you could create who you wanted to be was revolutionary at the time. He and Sigmund Freud were pioneers in the early 1900s, when the scientific study of psychology was quite new.

The science of the mind is expanding as we grow with the digital age and artificial intelligence. I predict this area of science is going to boom in the future. One way it is already taking off is with online learning at school. The switch to digital was a little rough and unexpected, but we have to learn to use it. I know this is going to be a real game changer because ANYTHING you want to learn is at your fingertips. You can be anything – go for it!

Day 19 - My Family Ties

Warm-up Questions:

1. Describe the type of family you come from.
2. What kind of values did your family teach you?
3. What habits or traditions did you learn from your family?
4. Who in your family is encouraging your growth?
5. What do you dislike about your family?

Power Words: Family Values, Influence

Family Values: The traditional or cultural roles, beliefs, attitudes, and ideals that are passed down from previous generations of the family to their children.

Influence: The ability to affect a person's character, development, or behavior indirectly.

Lesson:

People often say, "You can choose your friends, but you can't choose your family". There's a lot of truth in that as we didn't get to choose whose kid we became. We just became aware of our surroundings one day and some people introduced themselves to us as our parents.

From then on, we got to see our parents every day. They helped us shower and bought our clothes. They helped us brush our teeth until we could do it ourselves. They made us eat broccoli, took us to the doctor's office when we got sick and taught us the first words we knew.

Our family unit is typically a home type place we belong to. We are the kids and the adults look after us. Sometimes, we are their kids by birth. At other times, our parents choose to adopt us or foster us. Whatever way the relationship begins, we are family, and our family loves us. Sometimes family relationships aren't always perfect. Many times, we get our earliest happy memories and saddest memories from our families. But that's what we've got.

Our earliest influences, knowledge and habits come from our family. This is because a lot of the things we have learned can be traced to the family we belong to. Good families influence you in the positive direction. There, you are able to pick up habits that will push you in the direction of your goals and your future.

But bad families do the same thing. They teach you the wrong kinds of values; show you bad habits that can set you on a destructive path. It takes extreme effort to break the cycle of generational failure.

Some people are lucky enough to be a part of families that teach the right things, but others aren't. When you grow up in an environment that is hostile and doesn't support growth or progress, you have to choose to see and do things differently. It's a lot harder when this happens because our families are supposed to show us good examples and expose us to the right kind of values from the start.

But if they haven't done a good job, you have to take responsibility for yourself and decide to do things differently so that you will have a successful future. To do this, you have to discard the negative values you grew up with and pick up the positive ones we've talked about.

If you were lucky enough to be born into a family that taught you good values, but you lost your way, retrace your steps and pick those values up again. Part of growing up is realizing the right thing and choosing to do it.

What if my family is not the greatest?

When you're able to pinpoint and understand how much influence your family has had on you, it's easier to know why you have turned out the way you did. Of course, a lot of times, we are influenced by other people outside the family unit. But our earliest and deepest values come from the families we belong to. It's always best to recognize it and embrace them if they're positive or discard them if they're not.

I just want you to know about the influences people have over each other, beginning at birth. Sometimes you have to create a new family. There is not a rule saying, "family is only blood". Lots of people build a family with people they love and want to share life with. Everyone deserves a peaceful home and caring people around, if you need help making that happen, just ask.

DAY 19 - MY FAMILY TIES

Exercise #1 - What Are My Family Values?

Look back at your notes about your feelings and which values you hold dear. Today I want you to identify values you have learned from your family and those you disagree with, if any. This is a look-back at where the values came from. What traditions or family bonding activities do you do and do they all benefit you?

In my family, we value ...

We are particular about ...

I disagree with (describe the values you disagree with and why) ...

Exercise #2 - Where Are My Family Roots?

We might not always recognize our family's heritage as part of who we are, but it is. Our cultural fabric is made up of special recipes and holiday traditions passed down from generations. Take time to talk with your family about the past and where you come from. Ask about relatives, graduations and overcoming hardships. Fill in these sentence starters with background info and I bet you will appreciate a few more of your roots.

My mom/dad came from _____ and they do _____ for work.

My grandparents came from _____ and they used to _____.

My family faced a challenge of _____ but then this happened _____.

My most successful relative is _____ because _____

My best holiday memory is of _____

Today's Scorecard

1 Point for Each	Diet - Fitness - Water - Sleep - Attendance - Gratitude	
2 Points for Each	Attitude - Schoolwork - Warm-up Questions	**Add It Up!**
5 Points for Each	Daily Exercises	
10 Points	SMART Wakeup	
BONUS Points	SMART Tasks	

DEPOSIT TOTAL FOR TODAY

MY POINTS =

Social Media Boost - Bonus 10+ points

Take a fun family photo and share it on your favorite social media platform. Showing off your family heritage is a real ego booster because you gain confidence and self-worth with every positive energy message you post. Be sure to upload to the websites: SmartStartChallenge.com and AskMsPeck.com.

Coaching Tip From Ms. Peck —

Another beautiful day is ahead tomorrow. Take an extra minute for gratitude and spirituality. Write a quick thank you to yourself for the self care and post it. We can get so focused on today or tomorrow that we forget to enjoy life along the way. The more you learn about the world, hopefully, the more you will appreciate everything we have here. Exhale and say thanks.

Day 20 - Friendship Is Like A Mirror

Warm-up Questions:

1. What kind of friends do you have?
2. Do you have a girl/boyfriend?
3. Do you have personal boundaries with your friends?
4. What do you and your friends talk about?
5. Do you have a best friend? What makes them special?

Power Words: Friends, Romance

Friends: People who you know well and who you like a lot, not a member of your family.

Romance: An emotional feeling of love for, or a strong attraction towards another person.

Lesson:

Your choice of friends says a lot about the kind of person you are and will turn out to be. There's an old proverb that goes, "Show me your friends and I'll tell you who you are". The proverb is saying people in the same category tend to hang out together.

People who have nothing in common usually find it difficult to associate with each other. Think about it in your life and the people you call friends. So, is it safe to say that the people you let into your circle are people just like you, or who you want to be like?

Friendship is like a mirror because it reflects who you are and what you are about.

Making friends is a really huge part of growing up. This is because friends influence us. Our choice of friends affects our life's journey to a great degree. They influence our choices and decisions by the words they say and the things they do.

When you are friends with someone, you want them to see you as cool. You'd always want to win their favor or gain their approval. So, they tend to inspire or motivate you. Your peers could motivate you to do something positive. They could motivate you to study harder for exams or put in extra time for sports practice. They could inspire you to work harder at your goals. But peer influence can be negative too.

Your friends could persuade you to try out things you shouldn't. They could pressure you into going to places that you shouldn't. They could inspire you to adopt wrong habits like: skipping classes, ditching your schoolwork, drinking alcohol, wild partying, and drugs and so on.

Friends like these are the wrong kind. I am even going to tell you they are toxic. You should stay as far away as possible from them. They will bring you nothing but trouble and they can take you as far away from your goals as possible.

Toxic friends may seem cool or popular, but you shouldn't fall for that temptation. They're not worth it because they're not going in the same direction as you. Your destination is success. They are heading toward failure and doom.

Romance is another thing that affects you more than people may be willing to admit. A lot of the time, there's someone you have feelings for. They don't know about it. You are shy to tell them because you're scared that they don't feel the same way. They won't look in your direction and you wish they would, even if it's just for a minute. You think about them every time of every day.

Maybe you are also ashamed to talk to anyone about it. First of all, you shouldn't be ashamed. You should realize that feelings are natural. You were born with them. So, it's normal to have those feelings for that boy or girl. But you should also understand that what makes us a lot different from animals is, we don't always act on our feelings. That is because we have values.

As people who have a clear path ahead of us, we choose to cultivate discipline and self-control. We can choose to focus on what's important and then your feelings will sort themselves out. Even when the person you care about feels the same way, you can choose to hang out with them. But don't let it get complicated with sex or spending too much time together.

Remember that you have a goal, things you want to achieve and a life ahead of you. If the person or people you're hanging out with are neither motivating you nor working on their lives, you shouldn't be hanging out with them. I'm sorry, but every minute is important and wasting time and energy on less than desirable people only hurts you. Start being SMARTER about who you consider a friend.

DAY 20 - FRIENDSHIP IS LIKE A MIRROR

Exercise #1 - Upgrade Your Friendships

We've talked about different kinds of friends and it is time to get yours in tip-top condition. Take an inventory of your "real people" friend list below and then and rate them on a scale of 1-10: 1 for those who don't encourage you or inspire positive behaviors and 10 for those who do a really great job at it. *** This is a good time to have a conversation with those low scoring friends and explain how you are thinking and ask them to join you in the SMART START CHALLENGE, because you are about to cut the bad ones loose.

I also want you to take stock of how you act as a friend.

Do you encourage and support your friends? I know you will adjust your behavior to be the type of friend you want to have. Be smarter and pro-active, when you make the first move you often get the first prize. Consider how to use your new brainpower to improve your friendships. Go, do it.

My Friend List:	What Challenge Are They Facing?	How Can I Be A GOOD Friend?

Exercise #2 - Setting Boundaries

A person really needs to have some personal space and privacy every day. You also need time for your studies and things you want to do like your hobbies and even friendships. It is important to make a schedule for your life and follow it. When you prioritize the important parts of your life, it is easy to be successful because you have time to work on it.

During those "me times", stay away from your phone. Be unavailable to friends and people apart from your immediate family. Let them know that those times they shouldn't call/text or visit (because you wouldn't be able to respond immediately).

It is good to let other people know when they do something you like. It makes them want to do more. It is also good to let them know when they do things to displease you, or make you uncomfortable. Most people want to correct a situation and remain friends, or become even better friends. To practice having this type of conversation, focus on their behavior that you did not like and how it made you feel. When you did ----, I felt ----. Open communication is necessary for friendship to grow.

Setting boundaries is a necessary part of every relationship. Always let people know what you expect from them and what you do not. Also, set boundaries as regards to your personal effects like your phone, your laptop, your clothes and so on.

And, I also want to remind you that physical boundaries with people are important to establish before you get into uncomfortable situations. Let people know that they can't/shouldn't touch you inappropriately even if you're in a relationship with them. Since you do not need any messy entanglements, you should set boundaries early on.

Think about a few boundaries you might need to set in your relationships. Explain what the problem is and how you can find common ground and set a boundary. Most of the time, you will not want to break the relationship up and an honest conversation works. Use your skills of looking at the situation from their side. What can you do to find an acceptable boundary?

Here are two examples of the need for a boundary. It takes a little bit of planning, or thinking when you need to handle a difficult situation. While you should learn from experience, you can not assume everyone will act or react the same way. They say fences make good neighbors because you know exactly where the yard ends. It does not have to be a "major thing", just something to protect you, your stuff and your feelings.

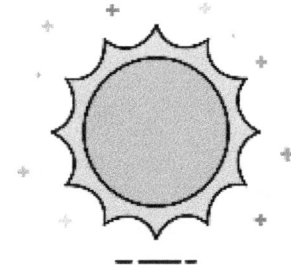

DAY 20 - FRIENDSHIP IS LIKE A MIRROR

Friend	Boundary Needed	Steps to Make It Happen
Joe	Used my video camera and did not return it for 2 weeks. He was mad that I asked for it back.	Next time anybody borrows anything I need to confirm when it will be returned.
Olivia	Too clingy - Expects me to be at her side every minute of the day.	Talk with her about how I am now focused on school and do not have that much social time. Ask if she wants to study together at the library.

Ok, now it is your turn. Think about those times when your friends and you were not thinking the same way. One of those circumstances that caused some bad feelings and you said, I'm never doing that again. This topic has even broken up some friendships over this years. Well, think about it – was there something to prevent it from happening again? Make a list of friend problems and create a boundary to make a better relationship in the long run.

These Friends...	Need These Boundaries...	Steps To Take...

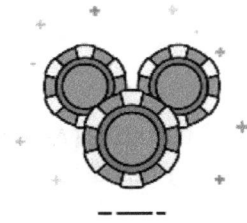

Today's Scorecard

1 Point for Each	Diet - Fitness - Water - Sleep - Attendance - Gratitude	
2 Points for Each	Attitude - Schoolwork - Warm-up Questions	**Add It Up!**
5 Points for Each	Daily Exercises	
10 Points	SMART Wakeup	DEPOSIT TOTAL FOR TODAY
BONUS Points	SMART Tasks	MY POINTS =

Coaching Tip From Ms. Peck –

Sometimes, you have to push yourself to step out of that box and rise to the occasion. Every day you practice these exercises is making it easier for you to push past those hurdles. Mind, body and spirit work together and create amazing things in your future. Push yourself. You can reach the stars in your future!

I also want to encourage you with your use of figurative language. I slipped in a few examples today and I hope you see how it makes an extra hidden meaning to the reader. It is a great skill to be able to recognize when an author uses a metaphor like these or times when emotional wording creates a big reaction. The more you practice using figurative language, the easier it becomes and your communications will improve. Just wanted you to know there are lots of examples in the handbook, can you find them all?

Day 21 - With Age Comes Wisdom

Warm-up Questions:

1. Have you ever had a long conversation with someone older than you?
2. What is your opinion about older people? Explain with examples
3. Have you recognized a role model in your life?
4. What do you think about your teachers?
5. Do you have younger brothers or sisters that look up to you?

Power Words: Role Model, Resource

Role Model: A person whose behavior, example, or success is or can be emulated or followed by others.

Resource: A stock or supply of money, materials, staff or other assets that can be used by a person to complete a project or run an business operation.

Lesson:

Many times, teens love to stay away from people a lot older than them. Sometimes, it's with good reason – some older people are not easy to relate with. But sometimes, there is really no reason to stay away. This applies not only to teachers or coaches, but also friends of your family, ministers and mentors. You think they wouldn't want a teenager anywhere near them but it's just you are being skeptical for no real reason.

One of the things that can help you become the best version of yourself is recognizing and accepting people who can help you. Older people can be assets. Many of them possess a wealth of experience and information that can help you. The things they know can guide you on your journey and the things they have experienced can keep you from making unnecessary mistakes.

Even if it is an older brother or sister, they can have valuable experience to share. They just went through these same "tough years" and they survived it. Any tips or helpful information should always be considered with regard to the source, but an "older person" does not always mean 20+ years older.

Find a mentor or coach like Ms. Peck to boost your success.

Everyone older than you – who isn't a criminal or a pervert, can be a resource. By that I mean, they can all contribute in one way or another toward helping you succeed in your life. Look around you, your teachers, your guidance counselor, your gym teacher, your coach. They all have something they can offer you. They could help keep you accountable to the new goals you have for yourself. They could also push you to reach milestones you never thought you would. They could give you helpful life tips and walk you through their past experiences.

The best way to develop a relationship with older people is to respect them. First, you have to realize that they have worlds of experience you have never had. Then, you have to recognize that you are the one who needs them. This is not exactly a friendship but a mentoring relationship. You need their wealth of experience and their candid advice and opinion.

To be completely honest, this type of relationship goes beyond what older people typically expect from teenagers. So, you should treasure it, be grateful and never take it for granted. Knowing that it's you who will benefit from the relationship will help condition your mind and help you treat them with the highest form of regard. It would also endear them to you and make them willing to guide you and share their wisdom.

As you talk with them, always be nice and polite and respect their boundaries. You can't expect them to always be available because they too need their privacy. They have families, hobbies, responsibilities, jobs and so on.

When you get to sit with them, it's smarter to listen to them more than you choose to talk. Remember, they are the resource not you. Your goal in the relationship is to learn as much as you can, so just listen and ask questions where you need clarification.

Be polite when you disagree or don't understand. Never argue or dismiss their thoughts if it's contrary to yours. Just learn what you can and separate facts from opinion – that's all. Remember, they are a guide not your rulebook. You want them to help you see the bigger, SMARTER picture.

Exercise #1 - Strengthen Family Ties

Do you have grandparents or aunts or uncles that have knowledge to share? It might seem obvious, but many family members want to help you but just do not know how. People can be so focused on themselves that they might not realize you need a role model. Consider someone older who knows about life and ask them if you could talk with them about your concerns. I suggest starting with a short time request and see if you can find new support for your new future.

- **Make a list of 2-3 people who fit this profile. Consider discussing this topic with your parents or guardian, they might know someone who is interested.**
- **Call them and ask them for 30 minutes of their time to talk.**
- **Bring a snack to share when you meet with them.**

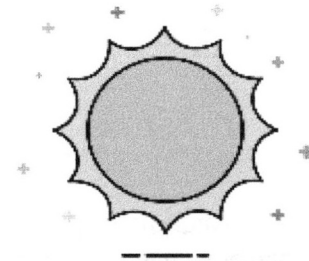

Exercise #2 - Take An Inventory At School

Which teacher inspires you most and why? Take stock of all the teachers at your school and think about the ones that have inspired you most, how they've inspired you and how much better you are as a result of their influence. As a teacher, I can tell you that I love to hear from former students who ask for my guidance. It makes me proud to know they value me as a role model. I am always willing to listen and give an objective opinion to students. I know most other teachers feel this way too.

Fill in the spaces and then go and say hello!

The teacher(s) that inspires me most is ...

They inspire me by ...

My Guidance Counselor ...

Media Specialist or Reading Coach ...

Social Worker or Case Manager...

Today's Scorecard

1 Point for Each	Diet - Fitness - Water - Sleep - Attendance - Gratitude	
2 Points for Each	Attitude - Schoolwork - Warm-up Questions	Add It Up!
5 Points for Each	Daily Exercises	
10 Points	SMART Wakeup	
BONUS Points	SMART Tasks	

DEPOSIT TOTAL FOR TODAY

MY POINTS =

Social Media Boost 10+ points

Take a photo at school with your favorite teacher and tell them about your SMART START CHALLENGE. Share your success with Ms. Peck and the world on your social media platform.

Coaching Tip From Ms. Peck –

Do you remember the children's stories known as Aesop's Fables? The stories were originally told by Aesop and written down around 600 BC, that is 2,620 years ago! One of my favorites gives some of the best advice for life. My tip today is about the story of the race between "The Tortoise and the Hare". One took every step with determination and focus, the other ran fast and wild. Think about who won the race at the end. Be like the tortoise.

Yes, that is an old story and today is about old people. Open your eyes and learn things about the world and our history. There are truths or rules about life. It makes sense to learn them and use them to win.

Day 22 - Setting SMART Goals

Warm-up Questions:

1. How is your morning Smart Start Wakeup going? Are you at 50% or 100%?
2. Who are your stakeholders and how are your relationships improving?
3. What does "success" mean to you?
4. What will you be doing when you will feel successful?
5. Have you started thinking about any short-term goals for the next 3 months?

Power Words: Goal Setting, Milestone, Success

Goal Setting: The development of an action plan designed to motivate and guide a person toward a goal. Goal setting can be shaped by following a SMART formula: Specific, Measurable, Actions, Resources and Timing.

Milestone: A stone set along the road to mark distance in miles, originally to Rome. Also, an action or event that marks a significant stage or indicator of progress.

Success: The accomplishment of an aim or purpose.

Lesson:

I hate to tell you this, but I think many students have stopped dreaming. For many students I know, school is like torture and they don't have any reason to think of any kind of future. They say it feels like you hit rock bottom or are stuck in a time warp of agony. If this sounds familiar, I hope the negative thinking has been turned around by now because you are in Round #4 of this SMART START CHALLENGE!

You are the number one stakeholder in your life.

In these past weeks, I hope you have been inspired and are taking control of your life. After you were motivated, you started dreaming and now you have your mission statement. By now, you are surer than ever about who you are, what you want to be, because you are making the right choices and forming the right habits.

You are also choosing the right kind of friends. I know your problems haven't all gone away. I know that sometimes, you may still have this nagging feeling in your gut. But I want you to hold on and be strong. Don't you let those problems interfere with your dreams!

Rather, surmount them because you have dreams – important dreams. They are important because they are the things you are passionate about and the things you are working so hard to achieve. Today, I want to remind you of what's important – YOU!

Your parents or family have their visions and expectations of you but what they want is not as important as what you want. This is the stage of life when you start to consider your dreams and imagine your future life. It is your life and you get to choose who you want to become because then you will work hard to make it happen.

When YOU make it happen, that's when you can say you're successful because you are the only one that can define success for yourself. So many times, people want to project their dreams, fears and obsessions onto you. Sometimes, they mean well but maybe they did not have the courage you do. They just want the best for you. But if their ideas of who you should be don't line up what your ideas, you have to discard theirs. Do it gently.

Learn to choose YOU over other people's opinions and sentiments. Choose you over their feelings, especially when you are sure that your choices are the right kind. Choose to do what takes you in the direction of your dreams. Those who are with you will get with the program. Those who are not in your corner will run off like scared cats.

You are in charge of your life. You can say that over and over till it sinks in. There's no one who has control over your life like you do. That is why you chose to make good decisions that help you become a better person and take you closer to your dreams.

In the same way, your attitude to your personal problems should be to overcome them. Don't let the problems get the better of you. When you set your mind to a problem with determination and thinking, you will find a solution. You're a fighter not a quitter. So, always see your hurdles as challenges you can tackle and win.

DAY 22 · SETTING SMART GOALS

I know you can reach any dream you can imagine if you create a plan.

Yes, you can be anything when you are an adult, if you think about it now. Set your short- and long-term goals and tackle them with grit and determination. An effective formula to follow when you write down your goals is known as "SMART".

- **Specific** – You must pinpoint the goal. The more defined the better.
- **Measurable** – Identify the results you want to achieve so you can tell when you have reached it or not.
- **Actions** – What do you have to do to make it happen? List the steps or milestones.
- **Resources** – Find the help you need to make it happen. Include your stakeholders and any service providers or materials you need. Make a budget and expect obstacles to get in the way.
- **Timing** – Set the calendar and make a work plan (graphic organizer) to help with accountability.

Here is a sample to show you how to start planning and breaking the goal down into easy steps and actions to complete. Any goal can be reached if you follow this SMART formula. I have added a blank plan for you to use now and a blank in the Equipment Room for use in the future.

In this example, the teen wanted to make a position on the school basketball team. They decided on the exact result they wanted to achieve and put together this plan. With a month to get prepared, it was easy to break it down into smaller steps for each week. They decided to break the work it into two basic parts – #1 Getting into condition, and #2 Practicing skills.

Then, those two parts were further broken down into specific things to do preparing for the tryout. These steps can be broken down even more, daily and even hourly for some plans. Next, identify the resources to help and the costs or expenses you need to cover.

Practice this skill by adding to the chart in the blank spaces under resources. Then include any ideas you would suggest to a friend making this plan. What additional steps could they take to improve their ability to make the team?

Specific Goal: Earn a place on my school's basketball team.

Measurable Result: Making the team. Guard position is my favorite.

TIME	MILESTONES	ACTIONS	RESOURCES
Week 1	Conditioning started	Start running daily Take measurements	New shoes Coach's training plan
Week 2	Focus on nutrition 100% Free throws	Go to bed earlier Serious ball time	Ask mom about protein for shakes
Week 3	100% Shooting drills	Setup court time with friends Get homework and grades under control	Coach? Check at school
Week 4	Basketball season starts with tryouts	Early to bed Pack gym bag	Talk to mom about extra snacks and the celebration when I get to pick my number.
Week 5	Team is selected	Yes - schedule practice into life No - consider equipment manager job	Celebrate for making it, or just for trying out!

DAY 22 - SETTING SMART GOALS

Exercise #1 - Goal Setting - SMART Task

Write one SMART, short-term goal for yourself to meet in the next 30 days.

You are doing a great job in this SMART START CHALLENGE and are almost done. Think about what you want to accomplish next month. This is a coaching day, so I recommend you dream big and really change up your future. Seriously, breathe deep and close your eyes – what do you want to accomplish?

Specific Goal:

Measurable Result:

Timing	Milestones to meet	Actions to do	Resources
Week 1			
Week 2			
Week 3			
Week 4			

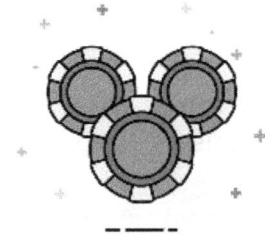

Today's Scorecard

1 Point for Each	Diet - Fitness - Water - Sleep - Attendance - Gratitude	
2 Points for Each	Attitude - Schoolwork - Warm-up Questions	Add It Up!
5 Points for Each	Daily Exercises	
10 Points	SMART Wakeup	
BONUS Points	SMART Tasks	

DEPOSIT TOTAL FOR TODAY

MY POINTS =

Completed Days 1-21 = 75+ Bonus points and the SMART Task 25+ Bonus points

Heads Up - Check off this SMART Task on the stats tracker

Coaching Tip From Ms. Peck –

A little bit of thinking every day builds up your brain power. Spend the time to get ready and meet your Catalyst for Change project milestones. Be sure you have researched your young people and their actions for change in their neighborhoods. You will be writing a script for your video in two short days!

Day 23 - Bring My Vision To Life

Warm-up Questions:

1. Where do you see yourself living five years from now?
2. What kind of things do you dream about doing for work?
3. Do you have role models that inspire you?
4. Do you know about the power of making a vision board?
5. What do you love to do in your spare time?

Power Words: Planning, Vision Board

Planning: The process of thinking about the activities, resources and timing required to achieve a goal.

Vision Board: A large sized collage of images, pictures, and affirmations of one's dreams and desires, designed to serve as a source of inspiration and motivation.

Lesson:

Think about it – without a map to guide you, it is almost impossible to drive across the state. Or think about the houses in the neighborhood or the cars and dresses you wish you owned. Without planning every step of the construction or manufacturing process, none of these things would exist. Life is the same way, no one can achieve anything worthwhile without a solid life plan.

But let's step back a minute and talk about the vision, or the dream. For a house, an architect has a vision before they draw a design. Will it be modern with glass or traditional with bricks? The vision is like an inspiration or fantasy for how it is supposed to be finished.

The dress you love was also designed by someone. They sat down and drew a picture or a sketch of what they thought the dress would be. Then, they thought about the materials and how to make it work on someone's body. Then they had to market it and sell it somewhere. All of these things happened because they had the vision.

A vision turns into goals and they turn into plans.

Close your eyes and imagine your life, let's say 10 years from now. What is that vision of you? When you are 25 or 26 or 27. This SMART START CHALLENGE is showing you how to make your dreams come true. Dream big and bold.

In life, our goals are where we want to go but our plans are what helps us get there. You can say a goal as much as you want but, nothing is going to change if there are no plans in place.

There are different kinds of plans. You have short term plans and long-range plans. Longer range plans are for the big picture or vision of your future. Each type details the necessary milestones or steps to take, resources you need and timing.

Let's say you want to be a medical doctor, for example. Your plans could be: I'll graduate high school, get a pre-med degree at my state school and then get into med school. That's long-term planning because these plans would take years to accomplish with lots of milestones along the way.

Long term planning gives you focus. It helps you know where you're going – your direction, and puts you on the right track. When you think carefully and make your plans, you should write them down. This can take some time to put together a detailed plan using a SMART template. You can write out a 5-year plan and then review it once a year and adjust accordingly.

Today, we are going to do something creative to get you inspired by your new vision of your future self. Putting your dreams and ideas into a tangible form helps make them come together and happen. I want you to make an arts and craft project but, believe me this is important.

Making an artistic project helps your brain realize you are serious. A vision board is when you take a large blank sheet of paper and draw pictures or print out pictures you hope to achieve in your future self. You put the pictures and phrases together as a collage and personal vision of your future. Then, you place the vision board where you will see it every day to inspire you to work towards who you have chosen to become.

DAY 23 - BRING MY VISION TO LIFE

Exercise #1 - Role Models For Inspiration

A role model is someone you look up to, they inspire you to greatness. Of course, many teens will say their parents are their role models which is a great thing. But many times, celebrities, athletes or entrepreneurs give you a boost when you think about their accomplishments. They could also be people from history or even fictional characters. Today, I want you to identify people who you feel have accomplished great success.

Once you have identified two or three inspirational people, I want you to look back at that list of values from Day #1 and Day #7. What values do you think you share? Close your eyes and breathe in their energy. What is it that makes them so awesome?

Select a few inspirational people and list the values you recognize in them. Explain your thinking.

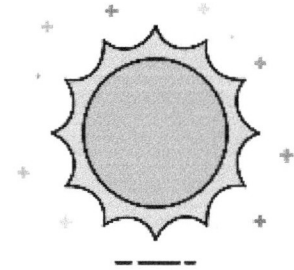

Exercise #2 - Create My Vision Board - SMART Task

Your vision board is a space where you can see your dreams coming true. In this exercise, you are going to be creating your vision board in any medium or style you choose. When I do this activity, I prefer to use a poster board and print pictures to cut and glue into an awesome piece of art. If I'm feeling silly, I will use colored markers and draw pictures that look like a comic book. There are websites or programs you can use if you prefer using technology. What matters is that you hang it where you can see it and smile, it will keep you focused on the bigger perspective of your future.

Decide which type of materials you will use and get busy making your vision appear before your eyes.

STUDENT SAMPLE TARGETS:

Today's Scorecard

1 Point for Each	Diet - Fitness - Water - Sleep - Attendance - Gratitude	
2 Points for Each	Attitude - Schoolwork - Warm-up Questions	**Add It Up!**
5 Points for Each	Daily Exercises	
10 Points	SMART Wakeup	*DEPOSIT TOTAL FOR TODAY*
BONUS Points	SMART Tasks	*MY POINTS =*

SMART Task - 25+ bonus points for Vision Board   Social Media Booster 10+ bonus points

Post your vision board and tag Ask Ms. Peck in your fabulous social media profile. Share your dreams with your friends because they will remind you when you need it and cheer you when you make it!

Coaching Tip From Ms. Peck –

William Shakespeare said, "There is nothing good or bad, but thinking makes it so." This 400-year-old quote is a reminder about your mindset and keeping your perspective in a positive direction. Your mind is something you can control and must control every day. Making a vision board and looking at it is another way you are becoming stronger and smarter. Brain training works when you practice!

Day 24 - Social Media Magic

Warm-up Questions:

1. What do you hope to improve with your Catalyst for Change project?
2. What surprising information or insight did you have doing this research?
3. What are the most important reasons to fix the problem(s)?
4. How do you propose we fix the problem(s)?
5. What is your call to action for people to do or follow?

Power Words: Inquiry, Reasoning

Inquiry: A process that aims to increase knowledge, resolve doubt, or solve problems.

Reasoning: A logical way of thinking that helps you form a conclusion or judgment.

Lesson:

When you began the Catalyst for Change project, you began to dig deep into research to understand a problem – in this case, a social problem. You asked questions, collected data and began looking for a solution. It was an assignment, but you did this to be a part of a much better world where that problem does not exist.

While gathering the bits and pieces of information, it is important to put them all together and make sense of it. You needed to learn more about the problem and how it affects people, here and around the world. From there, you are working with problem solving techniques and looking for any way to make a big change.

Your final SMART Task is to make a video that helps your social issue.

As a Catalyst for Change, you are going to make your case and convince people to take action and help you solve the problem. Since you have completed the research, you have to organize it or put it together in a way that makes sense to the people you are presenting it to.

At the end of the research process, you need to ask yourself, "What did I learn from this? What do I understand better? Have I been able to see how much this affects people? Did I identify the stakeholders and what they really want? What are the barriers? Where is the common ground? How can we achieve that"?

Ok, ok, I know I have not given a lot of details about the project because I wanted you to focus on the social issue and the research. Now that you know what needs to be done to make change happen, let's finish the Task due on Day #29.

The Catalyst for Change video needs to be at least one (1) minute long. We want it to go viral. Please be creative and thoughtful in your presentation. Include a strong call to action for people to do something to help. The video will be submitted to Ms. Peck and published on the SMART START CHALLENGE website.

I want you to understand that you have the power to create magic. Social media is an unbelievably powerful tool for change and your creativity and passion are like pixie dust for action.

It does not matter if you are on Twitter, Instagram, Snapchat, Tik Tok, Facebook or zippity doo dah - people listen to their friends online and you can cast a magic spell to solve any of our social problems.

Today, you need to start putting the research together and come up with something you think people could do to help. Your message could be greater awareness of the issue or a specific action you want people to take.

In calling people to action, you have to show them what's wrong, how you think it can be solved and how they can help. A good call to action speaks to our emotions and makes us want to do something to get involved. To get the perfect call to action, you have to present a convincing message that the opposition cannot counter.

This can only happen after you have made sense of the info from the WebQuest. Look back at your notes and ask, "What is the reason it has to be resolved?" This is the big "Why?" that people need to understand. It is the claim you are making in your presentation. We must do _____ because of _____. Decide on a reason of "Why?" it is important to solving the problem.

DAY 24 - SOCIAL MEDIA MAGIC

Next, put on your SMART thinking hat and let me continue.

Writers use rhetorical strategies or tools to persuade people in a logical argument. These 4 rhetorical strategies or techniques are over 2,000 years old so that means they work. The 4 ways of reasoning are like plays in a playbook in sports, athletes decide which one to use depending on the situation. Authors do the same thing.

Using these strategies requires critical thinking and judging the best way to make your pitch or call to action. Think about your research and the information that will work best with each strategy. Here are the 4 tools of reasoning - also known as F.E.E.T.

- **F = Use of facts, statistics or evidence**
- **E = Use of expertise, authority or firsthand knowledge**
- **E = Use of emotions to influence thinking**
- **T = Use of time, limited or one time offers**

These rhetorical strategies work, just look at any piece of advertising. Why do athletes sell trucks, or singers sell perfume? Because the marketing professionals know how to work these four strategies and make people buy things.

Authors use these strategies to convince an audience that there is a problem. You have to show them how much it affects real people. To do this successfully, you have to put up the facts and figures you pulled from credible or reliable sources – remember those good sources we talked about on Day #10.

The goal is to make your audience care about this problem as much you do. With your words, you paint clear and lifelike images that will get them to feel the impact of the problem. As they listen to you, they should feel like the problem affects them too.

Exercise #1 - Working Out The Reasoning

Before you start writing your presentation, you need to use each of these strategies with the information you researched. Go through each reasoning tool, identify the information you found in your WebQuest and explain how it could be used to convince someone to join you.

Always evaluate your information or evidence and sources. Always present the strongest reasons and look for the weakest in your opponent and consider crushing that. Seeing the evidence line-up will help you think and evaluate all of the choices or options.

Fill-in this FEET chart to help you organize the information you could use with each strategy.

Reasoning Strategy	Information to Use
Facts	
Experts	
Emotions	
Time	

Exercise #2 - Making My Claim

Look back at your notes and review the many reasons why your social issue needs to be fixed. Use your knowledge about teens in other lands and what they said about the problem. How can their experience help you better understand the impact on the affected people?

When you are making a presentation, the claims you make are different from just stating an opinion. A claim has to include the evidence to support what it says. Without the evidence, the claim is just hot air.

DAY 24 - SOCIAL MEDIA MAGIC

Here are two examples of recent environmental issue claims for you to consider:

- Greta Thunberg claims the governments' lack of action to combat climate change violates her rights as a child. She reasons her future is damaged and time is wasting. She calls on experts to share their knowledge and pleads with emotion for people to listen.

- Environmental organization Greenpeace claims recycled plastics are not properly labeled and are not actually being recycled. They reason the labels are not enough to encourage recycling and present statistics from landfills, evidence of low production and time running out described by experts.

I want you to underline the words "claims" and "reasons" in the examples above. Notice how the author gives evidence or examples of what they are claiming. Can you identify which of the 4 strategies the author is using? It is a decision they made when they were making their outline.

Earlier you identified the strongest reasoning to find a solution to your Catalyst project issue. Now, you have to write a message that gives enough information to make the reader understand the situation and agree with your call to action. The claim is the big reason why, it is often the damage being caused by little or no action.

- A claim must be arguable but stated as a fact. It must be debatable with inquiry and evidence; it is not a personal opinion or feeling.
- A claim defines the goal of your writing as well as its direction and scope.
- A good claim is specific and puts forth a focused argument.

Write down several claims for your Catalyst for Change project now and continue thinking about it. Brainstorm to get multiple ideas flowing onto paper. Use the samples above as a guide. You will consider them again in a few days when you start writing the video script.

_ _ _ _

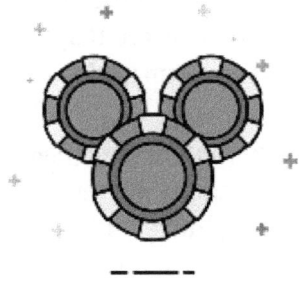

Today's Scorecard

1 Point for Each	Diet - Fitness - Water - Sleep - Attendance - Gratitude	
2 Points for Each	Attitude - Schoolwork - Warm-up Questions	**Add It Up!**
5 Points for Each	Daily Exercises	
10 Points	SMART Wakeup	
BONUS Points	SMART Tasks	

DEPOSIT TOTAL FOR TODAY

MY POINTS =

Organizer Bonus +10 points for Reasoning Strategy

Equipment Room Alert – Just a reminder to use the "FEET" organizer when you want to argue and win.

Coaching Tip From Ms. Peck –

Keep the four strategies ready and use them anytime you need to make your point and get people to agree with you. It is easy FEET– Facts, Experts, Emotions or Time. Take a minute and look at your research and evidence – decide the best tactic or strategy to use, and then put it into your most powerful words. These are the 4 keys to winning every argument and when you use them with expert skill, you need to speak up!

Day 25 - How To Negotiate Deals

Warm-up Questions:

1. What was your last argument with someone about? Explain
2. When you are angry, do you stop and think about the other point of view?
3. Have you ever negotiated to get something you want?
4. How do you decide what is fair?
5. Can you look at the other side of a situation or problem? How do you do it?

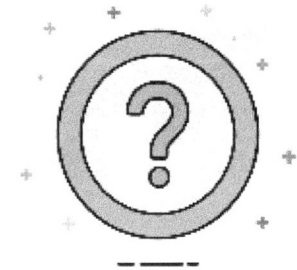

Power Words: Conflict, Negotiation

Conflict: A clash of interest, often called a problem. There are 3 types: man vs. himself, man vs. man and man vs. nature/universe.

Negotiation: A method by which people settle differences. It is also a process by which compromise, or agreement is reached while avoiding argument and dispute.

Lesson:

Conflicts happen every day. Imagine your mom wants you to clean your room but you want to play your video game. That is an example of a conflict starting to grow into some hurt feelings. Let's just say you continue to play the game and she gets frustrated and is not happy for a few hours. It might seem like a small thing to you, but they add up. Many times, conflicts cause disagreements and if not resolved quickly, could cause bigger problems.

Some people run away from conflicts. They are scared of getting anyone upset so they'd rather agree to everything anyone says. They think it's mature but it's really not. Putting everyone's needs above yours isn't always the smartest thing to do. Negotiating to find common ground is.

When you negotiate, something has to give so that you can have a win-win situation.

Rather than ignoring a situation or stomping your foot and getting frustrated, you can exhale, think and then try to reason with the other person. Ask yourself, "What does the person want? What do I want? Where can we meet halfway between each other and shake hands?"

On Day #17, we talked about finding some common ground which is very important. Today, you need to know that sometimes, you have to give up some ground to get some.

Negotiation is something many businesspeople are familiar with. This is because striking deals is one very important part of business. If you have been to a car dealership or seen a real estate agent selling a house, you would see a good example of negotiation. The seller puts up a price and the buyer tries to beat it down until they get to a point where both the buyer and seller agree. Then, they shake hands – a deal is made.

Now, let me remind you of the example above. This time from the other person's point of view. Your mom is trying to do the laundry and that includes getting your dirty clothes off the floor and into the washing machine. You are on a video game, again. She asked you a few minutes ago and you ignored her. She continued with the chores and cooking dinner for the family. A conflict is starting to brew because she feels unappreciated.

What if, instead... you remember tomorrow is picture day and your favorite shirt is dirty. It will take less than 2 minutes to grab all your stinky clothes and even take it to the washing machine to help your mom. You realize the game can pause for now so you can do the quick task. Instead of friction in the house, your mom is smiling, and you know you will look great tomorrow in your best outfit.

So now, let's look at this from the point of view of your social issue. Who are those involved? What do they want? What are the barriers? Have you carried out the research to know what works and what does not? If you have and you are convinced that you can find a solution, put your results together and present your case with facts and figures.

Don't be afraid to say what you want – say it how it comes to mind. As you put your desires, ideas and suggestions out there, listen to the opposing points of view. Don't dismiss them or wave them aside. Pay attention to their worries and fears.

Go over the facts and figures and find any common ground for both parties. Then, exhale because some progress is being made on the conflict. Continue to dig into those barriers, ask question, makeup scenarios - eventually you will reach a deal or agreement.

DAY 25 - HOW TO NEGOTIATE DEALS

Exercise #1 - The Heart Of The Deal

In negotiation, you give some and you get some – everyone wins. When it works well, there is no perception of a winner or loser. That's why it is important to find a common ground or a point where everyone agrees. When we negotiate, we don't get a hundred percent of what we came for, but we go home with enough to make us smile.

In this exercise, you are going to brainstorm about your social issue, identify the stakeholders and figure out what they want. Compare this list with the barriers preventing it from happening. The personal connection and emotions are at work here; listen to their heart and their words.

As you begin to create your Catalyst For Change video, this exercise works on your ability to put an idea together and propose something to help your social cause. I want you to find a common ground or way to help and write it up like an offer. Make it easy for the both sides to agree. What could be done to improve the situation?

Who are the stakeholders and what do they want?

What deals can you make for your social issue?

What can your side give up to get change started?

Exercise #2 This Time, It Is Personal

This time think about your personal/school issue and repeat the exercise. You probably need to put aside some hurt feelings and be honest with yourself. It is always good to start taking responsibility for what you do and what you say.

Being able to think critically about a situation shows how much smarter you are getting every day. Look back at your notes from Day #11 when you kept asking questions to get to the real problem you are facing. Now, consider both sides of the situation and find a deal to make.

Who are the stakeholders and what do they want?

What deals can you make for your personal issue?

What can you give up to get change started?

Today's Scorecard

1 Point for Each	Diet - Fitness - Water - Sleep - Attendance - Gratitude	
2 Points for Each	Attitude - Schoolwork - Warm-up Questions	Add It Up!
5 Points for Each	Daily Exercises	
10 Points	SMART Wakeup	
BONUS Points	SMART Tasks	

DEPOSIT TOTAL FOR TODAY

MY POINTS =

BONUS Overtime + 10 points

You can go and put in some extra time on your research. Look again for actions people are taking to raise awareness and drive change. What petitions need signatures or whose phones need to be ringing? Keep searching for a great idea to present in your Catalyst For Change video!

Coaching Tip From Ms. Peck –

Play every minute of the game. Can you imagine a professional athlete sitting down and taking off their shoes before the final whistle is blown? No way. My tip is to work on improving yourself every minute you can. Schedule your priorities and put in the brain power. If you want something, you have to be willing to do the work to make it happen. Don't waste time because you never get it back.

Day 26 - Put My Ideas Together

Warm-up Questions:

1. Have you ever made a video post on your social media? Explain
2. What is the most important thing people need to understand about your Catalyst for Change project?
3. Have you ever done a presentation at school? Explain
4. How can you make someone be passionate about something you care about?
5. What are your sources for your project? Describe their authority or credibility.

Power Words: Information, Presentation

Information: Knowledge obtained from investigation, study, or instruction.

Presentation: The process of explaining (communicating in an orderly way) a topic to an audience. You inform and persuade your audience with a new idea or a line of reasoning.

Lesson:

You have done your research and made some findings about the issue. You have collected data, gone through it and understood the direction it's headed. Yesterday, you were able to come up with your best solution as a call to action. The promotional video you are about to make needs to be made with laser focus and accuracy.

Your sources of information can make you or break you.

Now, it's time to make your point and be heard. What you want to say is important. As you state your case, be sure to present it with undeniable evidence and facts. People are skeptical about new information or things they are not passionate about. So, they want to know you're not making things up. That's why the places you get your information from are important.

When you make your video, tell us about how you gathered your data from respected news journalists or service organizations, or a government or university website. Tell us about the journals you consulted before putting two and two together. It will not only impress us but also, we will know that your reasoning must also be factual and sound, since your sources are credible.

Be careful not to arrive at the wrong kinds of conclusions. Don't generalize or appeal to our emotions when you're presenting facts. State it the way it is and then draw the right conclusions or meanings from the information you present.

What is the best way to make a difference in your community?

If you put some ideas together and come up with a new solution that people haven't heard before, some people may not take you seriously. But, if you tell them that a well-respected and well-known expert in that field said it, they will listen. It could even be a prediction that someone in the past made – of course, supported by someone more recent.

As much as you can, always refer to recent studies for information. I say this because new findings happen over time. Every day, new things are discovered. Researchers find out more things with the help of newer and more sophisticated methods of research. So, it's always better to talk about what is happening now, not what happened long ago.

After pooling the facts together and organizing them, you will start to write and draft your presentation. In your presentation, make sure you arrange your findings in a way that will convince people to appreciate what you're passionate about. Get them to care about this problem as much you do.

With your words, paint clear images that will get them to feel as though the problem affects them directly. Put them in the shoes of the people who are affected. That's how you get them involved and persuade them to take your side of the argument.

Think about how word choices are often used to create more emotion in the audience. Can you use figurative language or symbolism in your video?

DAY 26 - PUT MY IDEAS TOGETHER

You also need to consider the 4 different reasoning strategies and decide how to use the best your research in the presentation. Finally, you need to make the call to action of something the audience needs to go and do. Be creative in the ways you encourage people to get involved to improve the social issue. Remember, anything is possible when you have a vision and goals.

Many times, students tell me they don't need to make an outline and I shake my head every time and say, "Yes, you do". Trust me, planning now will help you write better later. It does not have to be complicated or super detailed. When you have an outline, it is like following a pace car when you are in a bicycle race, it sets the direction and focuses the competitor.

You have to get the SMART START and put your ideas into an outline before you start writing. This is also a check on your information and filling any research gaps, especially with good quotes from primary sources. Follow this guide to start writing your plan for your presentation.

1. Introduction - Identify the problem and make a claim or state the issue
2. Body - Tell the background story
    1. add facts from reliable sources
    2. add quotes from people involved
3. Pitch your proposed solution
    1. add details about it
    2. add benefits or common ground
4. Closing - Call to action or next steps

Exercise #1 - Organizing My Presentation - SMART Task

Get started here with this outline. Follow the guide above and put together your ideas. I always recommend you expand past this space and work on paper or laptop. If you work a little each day, it is impossible to fail. Ok, let's save the world – go!

Intro – 1.

Body – 2.

Pitch – 3.

Closing - 4.

Today's Scorecard

1 Point for Each	Diet - Fitness - Water - Sleep - Attendance - Gratitude	
2 Points for Each	Attitude - Schoolwork - Warm-up Questions	**Add It Up!**
5 Points for Each	Daily Exercises	
10 Points	SMART Wakeup	DEPOSIT TOTAL FOR TODAY
BONUS Points	SMART Tasks	MY POINTS =

SMART Task +25 Bonus points for Outline

Coaching Tip From Ms. Peck

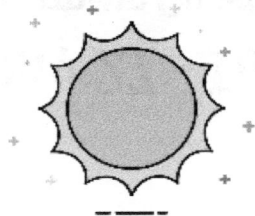

Take a few minutes today, to review your positive messages and internal motivators for success that we talked about on Days #9 and #13. Check yourself for any negativity in your words or spirit. Be sure your Smart Start Wakeup is supercharged, and laser focused on your success in the SMART START CHALLENGE and in LIFE!

Day 27 - Draft Day Kickoff

Warm-up Questions:

1. Do you have experience writing essays? Explain.
2. Have you considered the types of technology you will use to make and edit your video?
3. Do you realize that making a video script requires the same kind of organization as a written paper?
4. How can you be creative with your social issue video?
5. Have you looked for any young activists' blogs/vlogs to get a better understanding of the Catalyst for Change project?

Power Words: Draft, First Draft

Draft: A working version of a piece of writing going from first or initial, to edits or revisions and final publication.

First Draft: The earliest version of a piece of writing. It is a rough sketch of what your finished work will be like.

Lesson:

A first draft is the writing you do after getting all your facts and figures together in your outline. As you keep editing and going over what you've written, you create revisions. When you are satisfied with what you have written, you will publish it. Writing is a process and this is great practice working on something important in your real life.

Many times, people put a lot of pressure on themselves to get it right the first time. People also have this strong desire to be perfect and think their first attempt is best. Think of it as simply getting something down onto paper – it will get revised later, no big deal now... just write!

Every good writer will tell you the first idea is never the best.

I know everybody thinks they are a genius all the time, but that is just not reality. You can't make a good presentation, or do anything worthwhile, with your first attempt. With our first draft, we have a general idea of what we want to talk about and how we want to do it. Then, we look for ways to improve it with edits or making better word choices.

Here are some pointers. When you are drafting your presentation for the first time, write it like you're talking to a specific person in the room. This way, it's not boring and it would sound like something that can convince almost anyone.

Keep the language as simple and as straightforward as you can. Depending on your audience (which is most likely teens like you), you want to keep the big words down to a minimum.

Don't write something that would make you sleep. But of course, don't forget to incorporate the facts and figures, and add in any quotes from experts you found. Give us recent research information and also appeal to our emotions.

After writing your draft, read it aloud. Reading aloud helps you spot grammatical errors and you realize when it does not sound right. You can read it aloud to yourself and then practice reading it aloud to your friends. You can also ask an older sibling, or your parents, for their opinion. Go back to the text you have written and make it better.

Exercise #1 - Kickoff With The First Sentence

I have to tell you to exhale because you can do this. You have done the research and put together a great outline using great sources. If you look back at your notes, you should find lots of things to use. Ok, just sit down and get busy writing. It is always difficult to get it started but once you do, the words start to come easier.

Follow your outline and put your heart into it. I think it is best to just let it all out, put it all onto paper. Look at your notes and add great quotes you found in your research. Write and write and write. Then, put it aside for a while before you look at it and start to revise it.

The target script on the next page is both the guide and rubric for the SMART Task. One thing Nathan missed was a quote from an expert, but his script over-delivered with research and photos in the video production. I am looking forward to seeing your video!

DAY 27 - DRAFT DAY KICKOFF

STUDENT SAMPLE TARGET:

Hi – I'm Nathan and I am a Catalyst for Change here to protect our beautiful beaches and waterfronts. You see – we have to take action now to stop the threat of rising tides. I live in Florida and we have lots of storms that cause beach erosion. Every year my town spends money to dig the sand out of the ocean and bring it back up to a nice beach for us to swim and play. (insert pic w/ equipment) Our economy is dependent on tourism, so all the hotels need a nice beach. The problem is that the storms cause damage every year. It happens because we have taken land that belongs to Mother Earth. Seriously, what were they thinking with "land-fill" 50 years ago? How could mankind think they could create "land" and build hotels on it?? We suffer incredible losses (show Hurricane Michael damage) and the next year we start to dredge and rebuild again. It's not only happening here in Florida. It is a climate change emergency and we must act.

Rising tides are impacting millions of people around the world. In Bangladesh, the land is so low and the country so poor, they can not begin to defend against the waters when they rise. (show emotional pictures). Over 5,000 people die every year in flooding and millions of homes are destroyed, repeatedly. In Indonesia, the island of Java is sinking because of over-development and the government is planning to move to higher ground on another island. (show engineering pictures) In Java, they are building giant concrete walls to barricade the rising waters, an engineering feat that works for the short term. We saw in New Orleans what happens after decades go by and those concrete walls break. Yes, that is a solution but one that does not last. Hurricane Katrina was over 10 years ago and New Orleans still suffers from the damage.

One solution is focused on using the earth to protect or restore itself. (show pictures) In the Bahamas, they are planting under the sea with baby corals and grasses. This approach takes time to grow but it makes sense to use nature instead of concrete. The Bahamas have also increased their building codes or rules for construction. While they want hotels to be built, they also want to protect the waters and make peace with Mother Nature. This is an example of a balance between the need to make money and the need to keep the shoreline strong.

The debate about Climate Change seems silly to many people but the fact is we have environmental problems that we need to fix. The scientists can argue about why the water is rising, the reality is that the levels are going up. We have to deal with it now. Trees and grasses are natural climate solutions that are available and they need to be planted immediately!

Here in my community, the Tampa Bay Watch organization is planting oyster beds and working to restore our underwater grasses. (show picture) I volunteer with them and invite you to join me for their workshops at the Pier in St. Pete every weekend. They also take cash donations if you can't get your feet/arms wet working.

Planting seabeds works, this natural climate solution healed the Chesapeake Bay in 20 years with this strategy. (show nice picture) We need to do this planting around the entire state of Florida immediately. While we can not stop the waters from rising, we have to be smarter about where we build and do everything possible to help strengthen our shorelines under the water!

Exercise #2 - Make That Video

Ok, now that you have a script, it is time to go film it. Put your best YouTube or TikTok ideas and skills into making the video. Be creative and have fun. This is not about your camera or video editing skills, so don't make yourself crazy over the tech. I know it can be nerve racking, but I also know you can do it.

The clock is ticking but you have already done most of the critical thinking. Do not rush the filming, there is still time to get it right. It is due in 2 days, but you only need one minute to make it awesome enough to go viral, that's easy, right?

Today's Scorecard

1 Point for Each	Diet - Fitness - Water - Sleep - Attendance - Gratitude	
2 Points for Each	Attitude - Schoolwork - Warm-up Questions	Add It Up!
5 Points for Each	Daily Exercises	
10 Points	SMART Wakeup	
BONUS Points	SMART Tasks	

DEPOSIT TOTAL FOR TODAY

MY POINTS =

Coaching Tip From Ms. Peck -

In advertising, they say there are no new ideas - only new ways to spin things. Any idea can be used over and over, so do not get frustrated if you are feeling stuck. It is always a good idea to look for other examples and use them as a guide for yourself.

I suggest you watch some viral videos, or commercials from non-profit organizations and look for production ideas that work and use them. I named this the SMART START CHALLENGE because everybody loves challenges these days. It started a year or so back with ice in buckets for a fundraiser and now, it is everywhere. Kind of obvious, but you're reading this handbook, aren't you? If it works, why not make up a CHALLENGE of something for your social issue??!!

Day 28 - Anger, Anger, Go Away

Warm-up Questions:

1. Are you a short-tempered person? Do you know people who are?
2. What do you do when you get angry?
3. Have you ever hurt yourself or anyone else in anger?
4. How do you cool off when you're angry?
5. Have you ever heard about or tried Laughter Yoga?

Power Words: Anger, Anger Management

Anger: A normal, healthy response to a threat which may also be used for a constructive purpose.

Anger Management: Learning to control your reactions to the things or people that enrage you.

Lesson:

Anger is something everyone has or deals with. Some people, because of their passionate personality, seem to have a lot more trouble dealing with anger than others. There are people who never seem to get angry because they are calmer in their approach to things. Regardless of our personalities, we all get angry sometimes. It's natural. What is important is how long you are angry for, and what you do when you're angry.

When we are angry, our bodies and emotions flare up. Many times, we don't think straight. We are just so upset that we want to get even or hurt the person who has angered us. Anger can make monsters out of really calm people.

Anger management is something everyone should take seriously.

Anger management isn't just something for criminals or people who have had traumatic events. It's something everyone should know about because it helps us live happier, well-meaning, peaceful and fulfilling lives.

As a teen whose body is changing, your hormones sometimes toss you into a variety of moods you can't describe. There are days you're tickly and fun to be with. But there are also days you're edgy. Everything gets on your nerves. When someone hurts you in those moments, it's easy to flare up and do something you will likely regret.

Anger also makes people lose control. When you're angry, it's like you're no longer in charge of your choices or decisions. In that state of mind, you could say things you don't mean and do things you would be sorry for. That's not very good because as a person, it's always best to be in charge of and take responsibility for your actions.

I want you to know that it's okay to get angry, but never stay angry. Staying angry for long periods hurts your body and puts you under a lot of stress. In turn, stress affects your moods, gives you aches and ulcers. That's why it's important to snap out of anger as soon as possible.

When you get angry, remind yourself that you have to still be in charge. You can do this by talking to yourself in your mind. Call your name gently and tell yourself to get a grip and calm down. Today, you are learning some techniques of mindfulness because you do not want anger to control you.

To short-circuit anger, you can think of, or create, alternative emotions.

For example, I remind myself about a happy place or song I love. I hum a little jingle in my heart and imagine being at the beach until I feel a lot better. I will exhale slowly and imagine the sand and sunshine letting the new idea flow over me. I do this when I'm getting frustrated or when someone is trying to upset me.

When you stop and think, you are being smarter and mindful. Research shows that our brains can be refocused by shifting it to another task. This "shift" in your brainpower can be triggered by one of your five senses. Your brain can not be angry when you use your senses. Here is a list of the sensory triggers and examples you can use to stop anger in it's tracks. What else would work for you??

- **Sight – Look at pictures of kittens or puppies**

- **Taste – Start chewing gum or drink some juice**

- **Smell – Spray your favorite cologne**

- **Sound – Turn on happy music or sing along with a favorite song**

- **Touch – Put on hand lotion, clap your hands or squeeze stress balls**

DAY 28 - ANGER, ANGER, GO AWAY

Exercise #1 - What Will Soothe You?

Think about what triggers you or sets your anger on fire. If you know how to deal with your angry situations, you will be able to make them shorter. Take time now to figure out which things will refocus your brain so when it happens, you will be ready. Identify your positive triggers to use against the negative ones. Make your personal list of go-to moves here.

- **Sight**
- **Taste**
- **Smell**
- **Sound**
- **Touch**

Exercise #2 - Laughter Yoga

Another helpful way to snap out of anger is with humor. If you watch something funny or remember a humorous time, your brain has to shift and give up that negative thinking. Laughing produces endorphins and goodbye anger. With a little practice, you can build up your mental strength with this 1 minute exercise.

Laughter yoga is when you think of something funny and laugh. Big belly laughs - you can start going ha-ha-ha and then go faster, laughing for a minute. While it starts out as voluntary it soon becomes spontaneous or real.

To try this now, let yourself laugh out so hard and loud. Not just once, but over and over. It will feel ridiculous but just laugh for as long as you can. Repeat the exercise – how do you feel now? Next time lie flat on a mat on the floor and laugh. Laugh for 60 seconds or longer.

Describe your experience laughing:

Today's Scorecard

1 Point for Each	Diet - Fitness - Water - Sleep - Attendance - Gratitude	
2 Points for Each	Attitude - Schoolwork - Warm-up Questions	**Add It Up!**
5 Points for Each	Daily Exercises	
10 Points	SMART Wakeup	
BONUS Points	SMART Tasks	

DEPOSIT TOTAL FOR TODAY

MY POINTS =

Overtime Bonus +10 Points

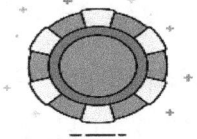

This is the last day to work on your Catalyst for Change video. I know you are not going to leave points off the scorecard. Put in that extra work and earn that overtime bonus!

Coaching Tip From Ms. Peck –

Every human being has an incredible mind that can discover or learn new things. I want to share inspiration from the most famous teacher, Annie Sullivan, and her blind and deaf student, Helen Keller. I hope you know the story of the child who was seen as wild to most people in the 1880's. Ms. Sullivan knew she was the only one who could help the 6-year-old girl. It was an impossible situation, but the blind, deaf and mute little girl learned how to control her mind and then control her world.

The teacher and student worked incredibly hard to beat the odds and find success. With a lot of practice and patience, Helen was able to communicate, graduate from college and become an activist for blind and disabled people. They say Helen never would have accomplished great things without Annie, but I think Annie needed Helen to become a great teacher.

I know I needed my students to help me write this book, without their struggles I could never help you get past yours. I hope I can be that great teacher for you. I hope you are learning that anything is possible, and you can accomplish anything you put your mind to. Helen did and you will too.

Day 29 - It's Showtime!

Warm-up Questions:

1. What have you learned from the Catalyst for Change project?
2. How has the success of your Catalyst for Change Project affected you personally?
3. What kind of a reaction do you expect from your Catalyst for Change video?
4. How can you build on your success with your Catalyst for Change video?
5. What have you learned in this coaching program?

Power Words: School Problems, Service Learning

School Problems: Issues that you are experiencing that affects performance in school.

Service Learning: A multi-step process that involves learning about a social problem, brainstorming with stakeholders and thinking up potential solutions to solve it.

Lesson:

Congratulations! I have been looking forward to seeing your video and I'm sure by now, you have successfully completed your Catalyst for Change project. I hope you're proud of what you've been able to achieve. Against all odds, you were able to conduct a research project and travel virtually around the planet. Today, you are presenting your Catalyst for Change video to the world!

Look how far you've come and see what you can accomplish!

Would you have thought you had it in you to work on a very important task like the Catalyst for Change and succeed at it? I bet you surpassed your expectations and I hope this makes you believe you can accomplish great things when you put your mind to it. You were able to put together something amazing and you have done a great job at it.

All this was possible because you decided that you wanted to win.

You won because you chose to solve a problem rather than whine and complain about it. Rather than ignore it, you chose to dig deep, brainstorm and find solutions. You looked at all the possible angles and identified the people affected. You found out what they wanted and you helped find a way to help.

I bet you did not know it, but you were doing something called "Service Learning". When you work on something important for other people, it teaches you something about yourself. While you were having fun exploring the world, you were really doing all these amazing things.

- **Developing skills in critical thinking, problem solving, leadership, decision making and communication.**

- **Building positive experiences with other cultures around the world**

- **Connecting your real-world experiences to academic subjects**

- **Strengthening an understanding of yourself and developing empathy and respect for others**

- **Applying your energy and creativity to community needs**

- **Increasing public awareness of a key social issue**

- **Making your voice heard and ideas known**

This was a difficult task, but you chose to do it and you nailed it. You worked hard at it and you gave it your best even when things got confusing and you weren't sure what your next step was going to be. Now, I want you to take that same attitude and deal with any personal problems at school.

DAY 29 - IT'S SHOWTIME!

School doesn't have to stink anymore because you can handle it. Like you did with the social problem, you will identify what you want – which I am sure is to succeed, and what's holding you back from attaining that goal. You will also think about the things that can help you tackle all your problems. You may need extra tutoring, additional resources or more study time.

For instance, if your teacher is boring, you could get fun resources in the library or online that can help you study better. If your math teacher talks fast, you could study the lessons before you come to class so that it'll be easier to follow when they start talking.

Choose to tackle your problems by setting goals that would help you achieve a solution. Set these short-term goals and ensure you complete them. Give yourself some rewards when you nail them and eventually fix your school problems. You know how to do this, go!

Exercise #1 - Publish Your Catalyst for Change Video - SMART Task

Send Ms. Peck your video so it can be published on our SMART START CHALLENGE website. Then, upload it to your social media and tag Ms. Peck and all your friends.

Exercise #2 - Finish Strong With Your Solution

Now that you are a Catalyst for Change and almost a Champion of Ms. Peck's SMART START CHALLENGE, it's time to finish this training program with your solution. You have learned so many skills and had great success with every practice exercise.

Spend some time looking at your notes from Day #17 and think. This is the last hurdle for you to get over now that you are at the finish line. Figure this out and make whatever it takes happen. You can bask in the spotlight because you have a plan and are smarter today working this problem out.

Define the Problem:	What is your position?	What is your opponent's position?

Who thinks this is a problem and why?

What are the barriers to finding a solution?

What do both of you want to accomplish?

What is going to be given up to make the common ground happen?

DAY 29 - IT'S SHOWTIME!

Today's Scorecard

1 Point for Each	Diet - Fitness - Water - Sleep - Attendance - Gratitude
2 Points for Each	Attitude - Schoolwork - Warm-up Questions
5 Points for Each	Daily Exercises
10 Points	SMART Wakeup
BONUS Points	SMART Tasks

Add It Up!

DEPOSIT TOTAL FOR TODAY

MY POINTS =

Bonus points competed Days 1-28 = 100+ points

✔ **Coaching Tip From Ms. Peck —**

Today is just the beginning. Those 100 bonus points are just the icing on the cake. You have made incredible steps toward a more exciting and rewarding future. Now that you know the insider information, you have that SMART START for high school and beyond. I know you are ready to face any challenge and know you can do it.

I love giving out awards and want to be sure you get the Catalyst for Change Video Winner badge. Feel free to post the badge with the video in your social media feed.

Catalyst for Change VIDEO WINNER

4 Awards Makeup the "Greatest in Entertainment" - 16 People in the World Have ALL 4

Congratulations to John Legend for earning this recognition at 39 years of age!

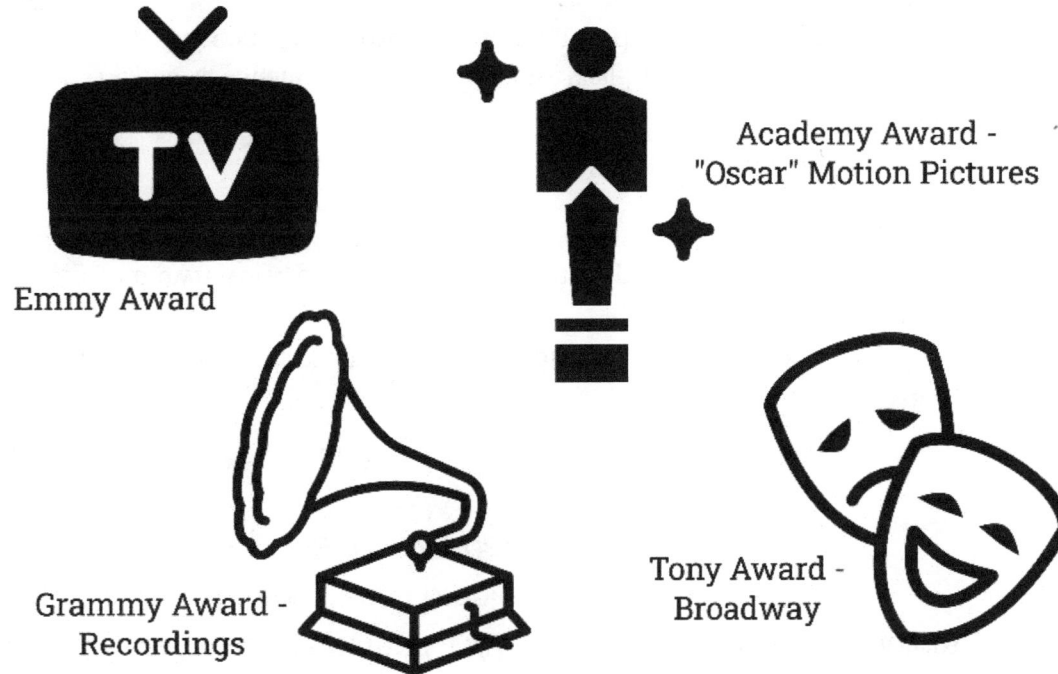

Emmy Award

Academy Award -
"Oscar" Motion Pictures

Grammy Award -
Recordings

Tony Award -
Broadway

YOU CAN BE ANY KIND OF AN AWARD WINNER -

JUST DECIDE TO MAKE IT HAPPEN!

Day 30 - Honesty Pays Off

Warm-up Questions:

1. What are you doing today to reach your Academic Goals?
2. How do you measure your progress?
3. Rate yourself on your performance in the CHALLENGE, from 1 to 100 points.
4. Did you make daily written answers and complete all the exercises?
5. What do you need to work on in the next 31 days?

Power Words: Goals, Self-Assessment

Goals: A goal is an idea of the future or desired result you envision, plan and commit to achieve.

Self-Assessment: Evaluating your own work, personal life and learning progress. When you grade yourself, you can identify your own skill and habit gaps and where your knowledge is weak.

Lesson:

Every fitness coach has a goal. The goal is usually to help trainees lose weight, become fit or attain a specific body shape. Everything the trainees do is aimed at achieving that goal. As the trainees undergo workouts, the coach assesses them from time to time to see if they are meeting their goals.

During midterms and at the end of the year, teachers give you quizzes and tests to assess how much you've learned. But, an evaluation isn't just something only teachers or coaches do. In daily living, self-assessment is just as important.

In any self-assessment, you need to be completely honest with yourself.

A self-assessment helps you answer important questions about your plans, your mission statement and the goals you have set. It helps you reflect on where you are. You would also measure how far you've moved in a time frame. These would be pointers that tell whether you are making progress or not.

With an honest self-evaluation, it is possible to know how well you're doing and what areas you need to work on. You need to look at your academic record and set some SMART goals. You also need to fix what you're doing wrong, or if you're moving in the right direction, how best to channel your energy.

Be sure to keep your growth mindset every day. We have practiced waking up and setting the focus for the day. A simple morning routine can establish the best attitude so it is strong, deep inside your soul. Little bumps along the way will not matter now with your new brain training.

It's not time to pamper you or pretend. You can't give yourself bonus points if you know you haven't changed at all in the past month. Self-assessment is a time to talk straight so that you can work on the areas that need improving. Self-assessment is a great way to help you stay true to your goals. This is because no one knows you better than you.

When you decide to motivate yourself, you are more likely to work hard at what you want to do or achieve. Journaling makes self-assessment a lot easier. When you write down your goals and write about the things you're doing every day, they become records you can use to keep track of your progress over time.

Exercise #1 Self-Assessment For School

What is your plan to get past the barriers in your academic or school problems? You have learned a lot of strategies or tools to be smarter and create the life you dream of. Take some time and look at the work you have been doing this month.

Look back at your notes for Day #15 and think about what you need to do. Fill in this graphic organizer to begin making a work plan for your next steps. This chart has your classes and focuses on your grade point. Set realistic goals and I know you will meet them.

DAY 30 - HONESTY PAYS OFF

	Current Status or Grade	Target End of Year	Actions to Make It Happen
English			
Math			
History			
Science			
Elective			
Elective			

Another area that might need a self-evaluation is any problems with discipline at school. Now you know about anger management and some conflict solving skills, what problems can be avoided or minimized using these SMART tools?

Exercise #2 - Journaling

This workbook has been your journal or learning log this month. Writing by hand in a book builds up your brain power with eye and hand coordination. Putting all these ideas down helps you keep track of what you are working on and keeps you focused on where you are going. Do not loose this momentum. You are on a growth fast-track, keep going!

I want you to continue writing your thoughts and plans down, so this is a shopping task. Get a journal or a notebook that you will use only for this purpose. It doesn't have to be fancy unless you want one that is. Personalize your book and start making entries. Keep it private and always be honest. Fill it with your dreams.

The Final Scorecard

1 Point for Each	Diet - Fitness - Water - Sleep - Attendance - Gratitude	
2 Points for Each	Attitude - Schoolwork - Warm-up Questions	Add It Up!
5 Points for Each	Daily Exercises	
10 Points	SMART Wakeup	
BONUS Points	SMART Tasks	

DEPOSIT TOTAL FOR TODAY

MY POINTS =

Coaching Tip From Ms. Peck –

I am almost done telling you my best secrets but there is one more you need to hear. There is another theory, developed by Edward Deci and Richard Ryan in 1985 about how people become successful. This "Self-Determination" theory states, it is in human nature to be curious about one's environment and interested in learning and developing one's knowledge. When someone has the freedom of choice and the authority to explore, they want to. When someone has resources of support and responsibility of a task to complete, they rise to the occasion.

Because of this theory, I decided to make my SMART START CHALLENGE to put you on a path toward success and away from whatever was holding you back. I know when young people have access to the world and a reason to explore, they are curious and want to learn. When you have this self-determination, nothing can hold you back. **The World Is Yours.**

Day 31 - Let's Celebrate Me!

Warm-up Questions:

1. How do you feel about today?
2. How has the past month been?
3. Do you like to celebrate small wins?
4. What do you consider a big achievement worth a major celebration?
5. What is a way to celebrate without spending money?

Power Words: Celebrate, Achievement

Celebrate: To acknowledge (a significant or happy day or event) with an enjoyable activity.

Achievement: A thing done successfully with effort, skill, or courage.

Lesson:

Have you ever seen a child take his first steps - maybe your baby brother or your little cousin? Everyone is usually excited, and they cheer him on. The first time he stood and fell, everyone held their breath in suspense. Then, he stood and fell again, and they all had the same reaction till one day, he stood and steadied himself. Then, he put a foot forward and then the other one followed after. He smiled and looked around. He was confident now. Everyone cheered.

All the love and support he got was more than enough motivation. Everyone's pride was his inspiration and because he wanted everyone to keep cheering, he got up just as soon as he fell to the ground. I imagine that this was the same for all of us.

Sadly, as we got older, things got a lot more complicated. Some people expect more before they can appreciate our efforts. We tried and tried, but it seemed that no one saw it. All they noticed was where we needed to do better, what we didn't do or what we should have done differently. Soon, we internalize these thoughts and we begin to treat ourselves the same way.

Celebrations lead to gratitude and long-term happiness.

Many times, we never get to a celebration of crossing a finish line and self-doubt creeps in. Often, it seems like things never end, or it is not a big deal worth a party. If this has been your story, I bet you usually wait to smash the big goals before you celebrate. And many times, you feel like you may never get there no matter how hard you push yourself.

The truth is every effort you make in the right direction is worth celebrating. You deserve a reward for every little goal you crush or task you complete. I say this because, these little goals put together will help you achieve your vision of your future. Celebrating your little wins motivates you to win bigger ones.

Today, you are going to celebrate completing this SMART START CHALLENGE. Against all odds, you have committed to a 31-day workout period of tough exercises and have seen it through to completion. You deserve all the points and awards you'll get today.

I trust you have been attentive, done your work with care and critical thinking. You have also learned a lot about yourself, your schoolwork and the people around you. So, take pictures, receive your awards with a big smile on your face and celebrate. You have done something great for yourself!

Exercise #1 - Celebrate The Final Score

Look at your Stats Tracker and re-check those daily points. Add the final 100 points for reaching this finish line today. Your final score is something to really be proud of. I hope you have learned how thinking will help you achieve the life you dream of. Every task you completed deserves a celebration.

Round 1 = _____

Round 2 = _____

Round 3 = _____

Round 4 = _____

Round 5 = _____

Grand Total = _____

It is time to have a good time and pick up your prizes. You have earned every award you get and I'm incredibly proud of you!

Today, you are a SMART START CHAMPION – and don't you ever forget it! Smile and Cheers to You!

Salute To The Champion

Congratulations!

You made it to the end of the SMART START CHALLENGE!

We have spent every single day of the past month working together making sense of the sometimes-crazy things in your life and in your schoolwork. Together, we have explored important topics that helped shape your identity, improved your problem-solving skills, helped you think clearly and connect with the people around you. We also looked at ways you could study better and improve your grades.

From day one, we talked about how important your direction in life is. We saw that knowing where you are going affects your choices on so many levels. It affects the people you spend time with, the places you go, the habits you cultivate and the things you are concerned about.

Every day was packed with lessons that inspired growth, development, mindfulness and having your own sense of identity. Throughout this workbook, we talked a lot about habits and how they helped shape our future. We also saw that what we put into things is usually what we get out in the long run.

Your attitude toward problem solving and anger got adjusted. We learned how to present an argument, how to connect problems with their real causes and find solutions. We learned how to relate with people, choose our friends and be a better friend. We learned how to set goals, how to assess our performance and to celebrate our little wins.

In addition to the lessons we looked at every day, you also had some challenging but fun activities with work you got to score for points. You had to do the research and inquiry, create the graphic organizers and even create your study area. You also had to get a journal – which I hope you will keep using because it works.

These activities or exercises were created to help you understand and appreciate the world a little more. They were also designed to make you think creatively and teach you how to express yourself. I was impressed by how well you did and I'm glad you followed the lessons closely.

I hope that this handbook has been a huge help to you. I wrote it with the intention of inspiring you and teaching you new ways of thinking about your future. I wanted you to see who you really are and who you can be. You are someone incredible, smart and able to think and come up with solutions.

I trust that you followed all the lessons carefully and you were able to understand them. I believe that you have been able to change your attitude toward your problems in this past month. I also believe that you have been able to adopt the good habits, strategies and skills in this SMART START CHALLENGE.

At this point. I have to be completely honest with you; 31 days are not nearly enough to totally change your life but it's a start. What actually makes great things happen is consistent practice of what you have learned.

So, to see lasting results or to get the most out of this situation, I suggest you read through this handbook again and re-do some of the exercises. Then, don't stop practicing the good habits you learned. Keep doing them. You have a SMART plan for 30 days, keep going and write a plan for this year. Planning helps you reach your dreams and give you that successful life you desire.

You have come to the finish line – every runner's dream. Somehow I know you are not going to stop here. I know you move on to set more goals and squash them. I hope that you overcame any fears you might have had, and you choose to live your life to the fullest.

Thanks for committing to this SMART START CHALLENGE. Thanks for trusting me with your time and deepest secrets. Thanks for digging deep and exploring your problems so that together, we could find solutions. I am incredibly proud of you and I hope that you are proud of yourself too! You are truly a Champion in my roster of students.

I would like to hear from you so call, text, tag me on a post if you feel incredibly different after this month. Feel free to say hi from time to time and share your successes and wins with me. I would definitely love to catch up and know what's up with you.

All the best to you always,

Mr. Peck

Power Words To Use

Achievement: A thing done successfully with effort, skill, or courage.

Anger Management: Learning to control your reactions to the things or people that enrage you.

Anger: A normal, healthy response to a threat which may be used for a constructive purpose.

Attitude: The way you think and feel about someone or something.

Brainstorm: A thinking activity where you try to come up with many new ideas. It is important to think in creative ways and never judge an idea while brainstorming.

Bully: Someone who is mean to others who are not as tough as they are.

Catalyst: A person or thing that starts an action - a spark starts a flame is the example.

Celebrate: To acknowledge (a significant or happy day or event) with an enjoyable activity.

Choices: Things we decide to do.

Common Ground: In a conflict, the small things we can agree upon even if we disagree on the larger issue or proposal/solution.

Communication: The act or process of using words, sounds, signs, body language or behaviors to express your ideas, thoughts, feelings and so on.

Conflict: A clash of interest. There are 3 types: man vs. himself, man vs. man and man vs. nature/universe.

Critical Thinking: Analyzing and evaluating issues objectively to form a judgment.

Direction: The course or path on which something is moving or pointing towards.

Draft: A working version of a piece of writing going from first or initial, to edits or revisions and final publication.

Dreams: Imagination of the future, or things you really want to have or achieve.

Expectations: A belief that something will happen or is likely to happen.

External Motivators: These are external rewards like money, fame, grades, and praise that motivate you to accomplish something, complete a task or achieve a goal.

Fact: A piece of information that can be proven true or accurate.

Family Values: traditional or cultural roles, beliefs, attitudes, and ideals. They are often passed down from previous generations of the family.

First Draft: The very first version of a piece of writing. It is a rough sketch of what your finished work will be like.

Friends: People who you know well and who you like a lot, not a member of your family.

Goal Setting: The development of an action plan designed to motivate and guide a person toward a goal. Goal setting can be shaped by following a SMART formula: Specific, Measurable, Actions, Resources and Timing.

Goals: A goal is an idea of the future or desired result you envision, plan and commit to achieve.

Gossip: A person who often talks about the private details of other people's lives. It also means a rumor or report of an intimate nature.

Growth: The process of growing or progressive development.

Habit: Something that a person does often in a regular and repeated way. It could also mean a type of behavior that is learned and practiced till it becomes involuntary.

Power Words to Use

Influence: The ability to affect a person's character, development, or behavior indirectly.

Information: Knowledge obtained from investigation, study, or instruction.

Inquiry: A process that tries to increase knowledge, resolve doubt, or solve problems.

Intelligence: The ability to learn or understand things or to deal with new or difficult situations.

Internal Bank: A term used to describe the habits and character traits stored inside of you.

Internal Motivators: Internal things like feelings/emotions, values, love that push us or inspire us to do something or achieve a goal.

Learning Styles: A well regarded theory explains how people will think differently when they gather, interpret, organize, evaluate, reach conclusions and "store" information for further use.

Meditation: A practice where a person uses a technique to train attention and awareness. It helps people achieve a mentally clear and emotionally calm and stable state.

Milestone: A stone set along the road to mark distance in miles, originally to Rome. Also, an action or event that marks a significant stage or indicator of progress.

Negotiation: A method by which people settle differences. It is also a process by which compromise, or agreement is reached while avoiding argument and dispute.

Opinion: A person's statement of belief, judgment, or way of thinking about something.

Outline: A list of only the most important parts of (an essay, speech, plan, etc.).

Personal Problem: The problems that originate within a person or their individual situation. These include a wide variety of financial, legal, alcohol or drug abuse, mental health, medical or family issues.

Planning: The process of thinking about the activities, resources and timing required to achieve a goal.

Positive: Something useful or something that has a good effect.

Presentation: The process of explaining (communicating in an orderly way) a topic to an audience. You inform and persuade your audience with a new idea or a line of reasoning.

Problem Solving: The process of finding solutions to difficult or complex issues.

Reasoning: A logical way of thinking that helps you form a conclusion or judgment.

Resilience: When a person uses mental processes and behaviors to promote or protect themselves from negative effects or problems.

Resource: A stock or supply of money, materials, staff or other assets that can be used by a person to complete a project or run a business organization.

Role Model: A person whose behavior, example, or success is or can be emulated or followed by others.

Romance: An emotional feeling of love for, or a strong attraction towards another person.

School Problems: Issues that you are experiencing that affects his/her performance in school.

Scorecard: A report that gives information about the progress of someone or something.

Self-Assessment: Evaluating your own work, personal life and learning progress. When you grade yourself, you can identify your own skill and habit gaps and where your knowledge is weak.

Service Learning: A multi-step process that involves learning about a social problem, brainstorming with stakeholders and thinking up potential solutions to solve it.

Social Issue: A problem that affects many people within a society.

POWER WORDS TO USE

Stakeholders: Those people who may be affected by or have an effect on a problem.

Study Area: A space in your home just for study where you have everything you need to practice and learn.

Success: The accomplishment of an aim or purpose.

Summary: A brief statement that gives the most important information about something.

The Seven Layers Of Why: A technique used to peel away the multiple ways someone has handled a problem. The idea is to dig into the root causes, motivators or actions for an issue and seek alternatives to improve future growth.

Time Management: The ability to use one's time effectively or productively. Time management is also the process of organizing and planning how to divide your time between your activities.

Values: A quality (of human behavior) we take very seriously.

Vibes: How your presence makes people feel.

Vision Board: A large sized collage of images, pictures, and affirmations of one's dreams and desires, designed to serve as a source of inspiration and motivation.

WebQuest: An inquiry-oriented process or research activity where the information you seek comes from the internet and a variety of websites.

Your Story: The things (experiences, habits, values etc.) that you tell yourself and other people.

Timeline of Knowledge and Communication

Over 4,500 years ago mankind began making symbols that represented ideas and later letters and words were carved into stone walls. Information was considered only for the people in power and used to keep poor people enslaved for centuries. With the birth of the Internet and digital technology, all of that restriction and oppression is gone. Everyone can learn and communicate ideas instantly. This is an incredible time – ANYTHING you want to know is at your fingertips – GO GET IT!!

First libraries of knowledge in Syria and Alexandria, Egypt around 2,500 BC.

Books are hand written, exclusive for wealthy for thousands of years.

Pliny the Elder, gathers knowledge into the first encyclopedia in Rome, AD 77.

First University opens in Fez, Morocco in AD 895.

In 1440, Johannes Guttenberg invents the printing press using movable type and paper. In 1455 he printed the first Bible in Germany and spread the info around the globe.

"The Relation" first weekly newspaper printed in Germany 1606.

Birth of the Internet 1992 with slow, dial-up service for large home computers.

Wikipedia, a crowd-sourced, multilingual, free online encyclopedia opens in 2001.

Mobile digital access to communications empowers people to over throw oppressive governments in Arab Spring of 2010.

Equipment Room

From Day #3 - My Internal Bank

Your body is a tool, and it needs to be properly taken care of. When you are aware of the care you give to yourself, you begin to realize how important it is. The simplest decisions about what to eat, or when to go to sleep can make you stronger.

Think about how many ways you can make those deposits.Good grooming tells the world you like yourself and adds fuel to your personal energy. Use this checklist to help get into the best practices.

- Wash your face, your body and your hands, often.
- Use deodorant or anti-perspirant to reduce odors and sweat.
- Brush and floss your teeth daily.
- Consider mouthwash and keep regular dentist appointments.
- Keep clothes and shoes clean and in good condition.
- Wear clothing that makes a good impression.

- Wear shoes that fit properly.
- Check your shoes for signs of wear and poor posture.
- Stand straight and relaxed with shoulders back.
- Keep both feet on the ground when seated and avoid leaning forward over desk or computer.

- Hair Care
  - Brush or comb as needed to look neat.
  - Style hair so that vision is not blocked.
- Nair Care
  - Trim and file your fingernails and keep them clean.
  - Remove chipped polish and repair promptly.
- Cologne
  - Consider where you are going and the impression you make.
  - Patchouli or Clove are never a good idea.
  - If someone 3 feet away can smell you, it is too much!

From Day #4 – Strengthen My Willpower

We learned about how important it is to have a strong willpower and not give up. It can be difficult to face problems when you feel hurt or treated unfairly in a situation. The point today was to decide that you WILL find a solution and use critical thinking to move forward. When you re-frame a problem and look at it from another direction, solutions will appear.

What is the problem?	**Who else is involved?**	**What is the conflict really about?**	**What have you done in the situation?**

Now that you are finished with the CHALLENGE you have more ideas and better skills than you did on Day #4. Keep working - the more you analyze a situation, the closer you get to discovering a solution. This is a decision process to get you heading toward success.

- **The problems I have control over are:**
- **The problems I can tackle by motivating myself are:**
- **The problems I may need help for are:**
- **The internal motivators that would help me build up my resilience are:**

From Day #6 – All-Star Student Success Survey

I originally wrote this survey when I started teaching 7th grade. I wanted students to realize how much control they have over their life on a daily basis. Because some of the answers are better than others, it makes a student think about what the "correct" answer should be. I hope this helps you consider what needs to be changed to improve your All-Star Student status.

Focus:

Do you feel you are eating the proper diet? Yes _____ No _____

Do you feel that you get enough sleep at night to be successful in school? Yes _____ No _____

Are you easily distracted or catch yourself daydreaming? Yes _____ No _____

Do you turn off the television or music when you do homework? Yes _____ No _____

Do you exercise or spend more than 30 minutes a day being active? Yes _____ No _____

Self-Control:

Are you aware that organization skills are needed throughout our lives? Yes _____ No _____

Do you know that setting goals for yourself helps you stay on track with life? Yes _____ No _____

Are you able to ignore distractions when they arise in class? Yes _____ No _____

Do you have rules at home with punishment or consequences if broken? Yes _____ No _____

Do you hold yourself accountable for the actions that you are responsible for? Yes _____ No _____

Self-Confidence:

Do you often say you can't or don't know how to do your homework? Yes _____ No _____

Do you feel safe and secure at school? Yes _____ No _____

Do you take pride in your clothing and appearance? Yes _____ No _____

Do you ask for help, or tutoring when you don't understand something? Yes _____ No _____

Are you willing to try new things or take risks? Yes _____ No _____

Study Skills:

Do you have enough time after school to work on homework assignments? Yes _____ No _____

Do you prioritize your work? (Most important or earliest deadline first) Yes _____ No _____

Do you complete your homework before you enjoy free time? Yes _____ No _____

When you do homework:

Do you have somewhere quiet to work? Yes _____ No _____

Do you sit at a table or desk instead of lying the floor or bed or couch? Yes _____ No _____

Do you have all the supplies you need to complete it? Yes _____ No _____

Do you have access to a computer? Yes _____ No _____

Do you use your agenda to keep track of assignments and due dates? Yes _____ No _____

EQUIPMENT ROOM

From Day #17 - Finding Common Ground

I think the hardest part about finding common ground is that you have to acknowledge the other side has something to recognize. Emotions get involved in difficult situations and can easily "cloud" your critical thinking. It requires you to stop and clear your mind to think with good judgement. It requires respect at a time when you might not be feeling like giving it. Exhale and think on both sides.

Problem: Dig into it and find the root of the issue.	What is your position?	What is your opposition?
Who thinks this is a problem and why?		
What are the barriers to finding a solution?		
Why haven't previous solutions worked?		
What do both of you want to accomplish?		
What could be given up or changed to make the common ground happen?		
Where is a win-win for both sides?		

From Day #22 - Setting SMART Goals

Here is a blank version you can copy and use over and over. This is one of the best tools I have ever used to reach every goal I set. Trust me, when you think about where you want to go and what you have to do to get there, it makes success easy!

Specific Goal:

Measurable Result:

Timing	Milestones to meet	Actions to do	Resources

From Day #24 - Social Media Magic

Here's the 4 types of reasoning you can use in any argument. If you want your opinion to have value, use one of these types of "persuasive techniques" in your presentation. It is also suggested you consider the other side and their reasoning. Being able to argue both sides demonstrates your critical thinking ability.

Pick A Reasoning Strategy: Facts, Experts, Emotions, Time

Glory To The Legends

Acknowledgements for Ask Ms. Peck's SMART START CHALLENGE

This handbook is dedicated to the practice of Cognitive Psychology and the scientific study of mental processes such as "attention, language use, memory, perception, problem solving, creativity, and critical thinking."

Many thanks to the amazing teachers I have worked with over the years, Mr. Sherman, Ms. Heuermann, Ms. Miritello, Ms. Lopata and Ms. Keyes. Much appreciation also goes out to the principals who coached me along my classroom journey, Dr. Shedrick, Mrs. Fuller, Dr. Peck and especially, Dr. Seuss.

Words cannot express the inspiration and motivation I have received from students in my middle and high school classrooms. I was determined to make this program because Marquis, Xavier, Beloved, Nathan, Dario, Melishka, Olivia, Jordan, Lauryn, Georgia and so many others who needed to know the real deal about getting ahead in life. Much love to my talented daughter Dorothy who has proven my unique approach to parenting (and teaching) worked and encouraged me to make this idea come to life. Finally, thanks to my mom, Cora Kent who has always been the greatest teacher for me.

Research Authority Includes:

Horace Mann * Napoleon Hill * Carl Jung * Abraham Maslowe * B.F. Skinner * Stephen Covey

Norman Vincent Peale * Tony Robbins * Howard Gardner * Robert Marzano * Dr. Harry Wong * Dr. Carol Jago

Evidence Based Practices Include:

Cognitive Behavior Therapy * Behavior Modification Strategies * Values Clarification

Self Determination Theory * Service-Learning * Social Emotional Learning * Cognitive Developmental Stages

Multicultural Teacher Education * Check and Connect, University of Minnesota

CRISS Project – Creating Independence through Student Owned Strategies * PEAK Learning Systems

What about the last word? Here it is!!

So while this CHALLENGE is over, the reality is another one is out there waiting for you to face it.
Thanks for testing yourself with this 31 day version, I am working on writing the next edition with 60
more days for a full semester of academic achievement. Ask me about it when you're ready!
All the best in the meantime, Ms. Peck

www.ingramcontent.com/pod-product-compliance
Lightning Source LLC
Chambersburg PA
CBHW080701110426
42739CB00034B/3353